D0500687

CH

Betty Crocker
4★Ingredient Dinners

- ◆ PREP IN MINUTES
- ◆ MAKE IT DELICIOUS
- ◆ EASY HOMEMADE TONIGHT

WILEY

Wiley Publishing, Inc.

For general information on our other products and services or to obtain technical support please contact our Customer Care Department within the U.S. at 800-762-2974, outside the U.S. at 317-572-3993 or fax 317-572-4002.

Wiley also publishes its books in a variety of electronic formats. Some content that appears in print may not be available in electronic books.

Library of Congress Cataloging-in-Publication Data:

Betty Crocker 4-ingredient dinners : from four ingredients to one great dinner / Betty Crocker Editors.—1st ed.
    p. cm.
  ISBN 0-7645-3892-6 (Hardcover)
  1. Entrées (Cookery) 2. Quick and easy cookery.
I. Title: Betty Crocker four-ingredient dinners. II. Title: 4-ingredient dinners. III.
Crocker, Betty.
  TX740.B515 2003
  641.5'55—dc21
                                    2003008733

GENERAL MILLS, INC.
Betty Crocker Kitchens

Director, Books and Electronic Publishing: Kim Walter

Manager, Book Publishing: Lois L. Tlusty

Recipe Development: Betty Crocker Kitchens

Food Stylists: Betty Crocker Kitchens

Photography: General Mills Photo Studios

WILEY PUBLISHING, INC.

Publisher: Natalie Chapman

Executive Editor: Anne Ficklen

Editor: Pamela Adler

Production Editor: Helen Chin

Senior Art Director: Edwin Kuo

Cover Design: Jeff Faust

Interior Design and Layout: Holly Wittenberg

Manufacturing Buyer: Kevin Watt

Our Betty Crocker Kitchens seal guarantees success in your kitchen. Every recipe has been tested in America's Most Trusted Kitchens™ to meet our high standards of reliability, easy preparation and great taste.

Manufactured in the United States of America

10 9 8 7 6 5 4 3 2 1

Cover photo: Fiesta Taco Casserole (page 130)
Table of Contents photos, clockwise from left bottom: Grilled Steak with Parsley Pesto (page 154); Home-Style Potato Soup (page 18); Baked Corn on the Cob with Herbs (page 178); Strawberries with Marsala Sauce (page 202)

For more great ideas visit **bettycrocker.com**

Dear Friends,

It's dinnertime. You're rummaging around the kitchen, trying to come up with an idea for something good. Trouble is, you only have a couple of apples, some brown sugar and frozen pork chops. Sound familiar? You're in luck. Because *Betty Crocker 4-Ingredient Dinners* was created to help you when you find yourself in this situation.

Inside, you'll find more than 120 inventive main dishes that require only four ingredients but provide big taste. There are soups, sandwiches, pastas and burgers, as well as skillet meals and casseroles. Something to please everyone, even little ones who can't yet count to four.

Other helpful sections include a Pantry Planner that offers tips on stocking up, **4 Star Ideas** at the beginning of each chapter and substitution and time-saving ideas in **Betty's Tip 4** You. After all, once you've adequately stocked your pantry, you'll need suggestions on how to use those ingredients effectively and efficiently.

If you're really short on time, go immediately to recipes marked **SUPER***Express*, which can be prepared in 20 minutes or less. That's faster than a trip to the drive-thru.

With *Betty Crocker 4-Ingredient Dinners*, who knows? Four ingredients could be your ticket to a fabulous 5-star family meal.

Warmly,

Betty Crocker

Pantry Planner   6

1 Supper Soups and
Hearty Salads   8

2 Pronto Pastas
and Grains   34

3 Sumptuous Sandwiches
and Perfect Pizzas   62

4 Memorable Main
Skillet Meals and
Stir-Fries   90

5 Oven All-Star: Roasts
and Casseroles   120

6 Great Grilling and
Bountiful Burgers   148

Table *of* Contents

7 Round-Out-Your-Meal Savory Sides   176

8 Finishing Dinner with Delectable Desserts   196

Helpful Nutrition and Cooking Information   216

Metric Conversion Chart   218

Index   219

Pantry ★ Planner

Stocking Your Pantry for Easy and Fast 4-Ingredient Cooking

Having a wide variety of food and ingredients on hand in your cupboard, refrigerator and freezer offers tremendous flexibility when you are cooking dinner. This pantry list covers all the basics of easy cooking with just four ingredients; feel free to add your own favorites to it. If you have a well-stocked pantry, you'll be able to prepare any of the easy 4-Ingredient recipes in this book—even on those days when you don't have time to shop. And even if you don't have all the items stocked, you'll still be able to make great meals from a partially stocked pantry—this book gives you great choices for a variety of foods.

Produce:

Fruits:
- Apples, pears, bananas, grapes
- Citrus fruits (lemons, limes, oranges)

Vegetables:
- Carrots
- Celery
- Onions
- Potatoes
- Ready-to-use salad mix
- Tomatoes

In the Fridge:

Breads and Dough Products:
- Pita breads
- Ready-to-eat pizza crust
- Ready-to-use garlic or cheese breads
- Refrigerated doughs (biscuit, breadsticks)
- Tortillas (corn, flour)

Condiments:
- Chocolate syrup
- Chopped garlic
- Hummus
- Prepared horseradish
- Prepared pesto

Dairy:
- Alfredo sauce
- Butter or margarine
- Cheese (grated, shredded, sliced)
- Cream cheese
- Eggs or egg substitutes
- Milk
- Sour cream
- Yogurt (plain, flavored)

Meat, Poultry and Fish:
- Bacon
- Boneless, skinless chicken breasts or thighs
- Deli meats (ham, salami)
- Fresh or frozen fish steaks
- Ground meat
- Ready-to-cook seasoned meat and poultry products
- Sausage (smoked, hot dogs, bratwurst)

In the Freezer:
- Desserts and whipped topping
- Dough (bread, pizza)
- Fruits (blueberries, raspberries, strawberries)
- Ice cream and frozen yogurt
- Juice concentrate
- Pizza
- Ravioli (cheese- or beef-filled)
- Vegetables (corn, green beans, any favorite combination)

Bakery:
- Breads (sandwich bread, rolls, bagels, hamburger and hot dog buns)
- Cookies
- Prepared cake (angel food, pound)

Off the Shelf:

Baking Basics:

- Bisquick® baking mix
- Cake mix
- Canned frosting
- Chips (semisweet chocolate, peanut butter)
- Corn syrup
- Dried fruit (cranberries, cherries, raisins)
- Evaporated milk
- Flour
- Nuts (almonds, walnuts, pistachios)
- Shredded coconut
- Sugar (granulated, brown, powdered)

Canned Basics:

- Beans (garbanzo, kidney, black, white northern, refried)
- Black olives
- Broth (beef, chicken, vegetable)
- Canned tuna and shrimp
- Fruits (cranberry, pineapple, cocktail)
- Green chilies
- Mushrooms
- Pasta, pizza sauces
- Soups
- Tomato products (sauce, paste, stewed, diced, seasoned)
- Water chestnuts

Cereals and Snacks:

- Bread crumbs
- Cereals
- Corn meal
- Crackers
- Croutons
- Tortilla Chips

Condiments and Sauces:

- Asian (hoisin, peanut, duck, sweet-and-sour and stir-fry sauces)
- Barbecue sauce
- Chili
- Cocktail sauce
- Honey
- Ice-cream toppings
- Ketchup
- Maple syrup
- Mustards (Dijon, spicy brown, yellow)
- Peanut butter
- Pimentos
- Preserves (jam, jelly, marmalade)
- Salsa, picante sauce
- Soy sauce, teriyaki sauce
- Worcestershire sauce

Dressings, Oils and Vinegars:

- Cooking spray
- Marinades
- Mayonnaise, salad dressing
- Oils (vegetable, olive)
- Salad dressings
- Vinegars (balsamic, cider, white, red wine)

Herbs, Spices and Dry Mixes:

- Bacon flavor bits
- Bouillon granules or cubes
- Dried herbs (basil, chives, dill weed, fennel seed, mint, oregano, parsley flakes, rosemary, sage, tarragon, thyme)
- Dry sauce mixes (cheese, gravy, white)
- Dry seasoning mixes (meat loaf, sloppy Joe, spaghetti)
- Dry soup mixes
- Herb or seasoning blends, regular or salt-free (Italian seasoning, lemon, Cajun/Creole)
- Instant unflavored gelatin
- Pepper seasoning
- Salad dressing mix
- Salt
- Sesame seeds
- Spices (chili powder, cumin, curry powder, garlic and onion powder or salt, ground cinnamon, ground ginger, nutmeg, paprika)

Pasta, Rice, Grains and Potatoes:

- Couscous
- Instant potatoes
- Noodle and pasta mixes
- Pasta (long, short and tube types)
- Potato mixes
- Rice (white, brown, long-grain and quick-cooking)
- Rice mixes

4 Star Ideas

Sensational Soups

You can turn a simple can of chicken broth into a satisfying dinner with these easy additions:

★ Add chopped carrots, frozen peas and cooked chopped chicken

★ Stir in instant mashed potatoes, cut-up cooked chicken and shredded Swiss cheese

★ Add diced tofu, dried mushrooms and rice vinegar

★ Add cut-up cooked turkey, cooked wild rice and a splash of soymilk

4 Star Ideas

Around the World in a Salad Bowl

Ready for adventure? Turn a bag of ready-to-eat salad greens into international salads:

★ Make it Greek by adding black olives, a jar of marinated artichoke hearts and crumbled feta cheese

★ Visit Thailand by adding peanut sauce, chopped green onions and strips of cooked chicken

★ Add chopped cooked pork, mandarin orange sections and ginger-soy dressing for a trip to China

★ Or take a gondola ride in Venice by adding canned white northern beans, red onion slices, canned tuna and balsamic vinaigrette

1

Supper Soups and Hearty Salads

🕐 Stir-Fried Beef and Vegetable Soup   10

Irish Lamb Stew   11

🕐 Chicken Cordon Bleu Chowder   12

🕐 Oriental-Style Chicken Noodle Soup   14

🕐 Spicy Chicken Chili   15

🕐 Easy Dilled Tomato Bisque   16

Red Summer Soup   17

Home-Style Potato Soup   18

🕐 Vegetable Chowder in Bread Bowls   20

🕐 Vegetable and Tortellini Soup   22

German Potato Salad with Brats   23

Florentine Salad   24

Quick BLT Salad   25

🕐 Canadian Bacon and Gouda Salad   26

🕐 Ham and Slaw Salad   27

Warm Hot Dog Pasta Salad   28

Zesty Pasta Sausage Salad   29

🕐 Chicken Salad   30

🕐 Tuna-Vegetable Salad   32

🕐 Warm Bean and Spinach Salad   33

Photos: opposite top: Chicken Cordon Bleu Chowder (page 12); opposite bottom: Chicken Salad (page 30)

🕐 **SUPER**Express *ready in 20 minutes or less*

SUPER *Express*

Stir-Fried Beef and Vegetable Soup

1/2 pound beef boneless sirloin steak

1 bag (16 ounces) fresh stir-fry vegetables

1 bag (about 7 ounces) fresh stir-fry noodles with soy sauce–flavored sauce

1 can (14 1/2 ounces) beef or Oriental broth

1 Remove fat from beef. Cut beef into 1/4-inch slices.

2 Spray 12-inch nonstick skillet with cooking spray; heat over medium-high heat. Add beef; stir-fry about 2 minutes or until brown. Stir in remaining ingredients and 3 cups of water; heat to boiling. Reduce heat; simmer uncovered about 5 minutes, stirring occasionally, until vegetables are crisp-tender.

Betty's Tip 4 You

Don't have time to defrost the beef? **Good news! You'll find that beef is much easier to cut if it is partially frozen, about 1 1/2 hours.**

Nutrition Information
1 SERVING: Calories 275 (Calories from Fat 25); Fat 3g (Saturated 3g); Cholesterol 30mg; Sodium 970mg; Carbohydrate 45g (Dietary Fiber 5g, Sugars 4g); Protein 22g

% Daily Value: Vitamin A 24%; Vitamin C 34%; Calcium 6%; Iron 24%
Diet Exchanges: 2 Starch, 1 1/2 Very Lean Meat, 3 Vegetable
Carbohydrate Choices: 3

Irish Lamb Stew

2 pounds lamb boneless neck or shoulder, cut into 1-inch pieces

6 medium potatoes, cut into 1/2-inch slices (about 2 pounds)

3 medium onions, sliced

Snipped parsley

1 Layer half each of the lamb, potatoes and onions in 4-quart Dutch oven; sprinkle with half each of 2 teaspoons salt and 1/4 teaspoon of pepper. Repeat; add 2 cups of water.

2 Heat to boiling; reduce heat. Cover and simmer until lamb is tender, 1 1/2 to 2 hours. Skim fat from broth. Sprinkle stew with parsley.

Betty's Tip 4 You

Microwaving will save about half the cooking time. Cut lamb into 1/2-inch pieces and the potatoes into 1/4-inch pieces. Place lamb in 3-quart microwavable casserole and omit the 2 cups of water. Cover tightly and microwave on High 6 minutes; stir. Cover tightly and microwave until very little pink remains, 6 to 9 minutes longer. Drain and reserve 1/2 cup drippings.

Arrange potatoes in square microwavable dish, 8 × 8 × 2 inches and sprinkle with 2 tablespoons water. Cover tightly and microwave on High until barely tender, 8 to 12 minutes.

Add potatoes, onions, 2 teaspoons salt and 1/4 teaspoon pepper to lamb in 3-quart casserole; stir. Pour reserved drippings over top. Cover tightly and microwave on Medium-Low (30%) 20 minutes; stir. Cover tightly and microwave until lamb is tender, 20 to 28 minutes longer. Skim fat and sprinkle with parsley.

Nutrition Information
1 SERVING: Calories 380 (Calories from Fat 100); Fat 11g (Saturated 4g); Cholesterol 110mg; Sodium 480mg; Carbohydrate 33g (Dietary Fiber 4g, Sugars 4g); Protein 37g

% Daily Value: Vitamin A 2%; Vitamin C 16%; Calcium 2%; Iron 24%
Diet Exchanges: 2 Starch, 4 Lean Meat
Carbohydrate Choices: 2

SUPER *Express*

Chicken Cordon Bleu Chowder

2 cans (19 ounces each) ready-to-serve creamy potato with garlic soup

1 cup cubed cooked chicken breast

1 cup diced fully cooked ham

1 cup shredded Swiss cheese (4 ounces)

1 Heat soup, chicken and ham in 3-quart saucepan over medium-high heat 5 minutes, stirring occasionally.

2 Slowly stir in cheese. Cook about 2 minutes, stirring frequently, until cheese is melted.

Betty's Tip 4 You

Add a flavor boost, as well as a bit of color, to this creamy soup by sprinkling each serving with chopped fresh chives or dried dill weed.

Nutrition Information

1 SERVING: Calories 470 (Calories from Fat 260); Fat 39g (Saturated 11g); Cholesterol 100mg; Sodium 1590mg; Carbohydrate 20g (Dietary Fiber 2g, Sugars 1g); Protein 33g

% Daily Value: Vitamin A 6%; Vitamin C 4%; Calcium 28%; Iron 8%
Diet Exchanges: 1 Starch, 4 Medium-Fat Meat, 2 Fat
Carbohydrate Choices: 1

Chicken Cordon Bleu Chowder

SUPER
Express

Oriental-Style Chicken Noodle Soup

1 package (3 ounces) chicken flavor Oriental-style 3-minute noodles

2 cups cut-up cooked chicken

2 medium stalks bok choy (with leaves), cut into 1/4-inch slices

1 medium carrot, thinly sliced

1 Heat 3 cups of water to boiling in 3-quart saucepan. Break apart block of noodles into water; stir in chicken, bok choy and carrot.

2 Heat to boiling; reduce heat. Simmer uncovered 3 minutes, stirring occasionally, until carrots are tender. Stir in Flavor Packet from Oriental-style noodles.

Betty's Tip
4 You

Want a bit of extra, authentic flavor? Stir a little sesame oil into each bowl of soup just before serving.

Nutrition Information

1 SERVING: Calories 225 (Calories from Fat 80); Fat 9g (Saturated 9g); Cholesterol 60mg; Sodium 420mg; Carbohydrate 14g (Dietary Fiber 1g, Sugars 2g); Protein 22g

% Daily Value: Vitamin A 64%; Vitamin C 4%; Calcium 2%; Iron 8%
Diet Exchanges: 1 Starch, 3 Lean Meat
Carbohydrate Choices: 1

Spicy Chicken Chili

SUPER
Express 🕐

1 pound boneless, skinless chicken breast halves

1 can (14 1/2 ounces) salsa-style chunky tomatoes, undrained

1 can (15 ounces) spicy chili beans, undrained

1/2 cup shredded reduced-fat Cheddar cheese (2 ounces)

1 Remove fat from chicken. Cut chicken into 3/4-inch pieces. Spray 12-inch nonstick skillet with cooking spray; heat over medium-high heat. Cook chicken in skillet 3 to 5 minutes, stirring frequently, until light brown.

2 Stir in tomatoes and beans; reduce heat to medium-low. Cook uncovered 8 to 10 minutes, stirring frequently, until chicken is no longer pink in center. Sprinkle each serving with 2 tablespoons cheese.

Betty's Tip
4 You

For added heat and flavor, **use Southwestern salsa-style diced tomatoes with green chilies or Southwestern-style diced tomatoes with chili spices.**

Nutrition Information

1 SERVING: Calories 250 (Calories from Fat 45); Fat 5g (Saturated 2g); Cholesterol 70mg; Sodium 1070mg; Carbohydrate 21g (Dietary Fiber 5g, Sugars 5g); Protein 35g

% Daily Value: Vitamin A 16%; Vitamin C 20%; Calcium 12%; Iron 18%
Diet Exchanges: 1 Starch, 4 Very Lean Meat, 1 Vegetable
Carbohydrate Choices: 1 1/2

SUPER *Express*

Easy Dilled Tomato Bisque

3 cans (11 ounces each) condensed tomato bisque or 3 cans (10 3/4 ounces each) condensed tomato soup

1 tablespoon chopped fresh or 1 teaspoon dried dill weed

8 slices lemon

1 Prepare soup as directed on can; stir in dill weed.

2 Divide soup among 4 bowls; garnish each with 2 slices lemon.

Betty's Tip 4 You

A grilled cheese sandwich, **oozing with melting cheese**, is the perfect partner for this homey tomato soup. Add a salad of crisp romaine drizzled with blue cheese dressing and a sprinkle of almonds for a satisfying, but easy, meal.

Nutrition Information

1 SERVING: Calories 135 (Calories from Fat 25); Fat 3g (Saturated 1g); Cholesterol 5mg; Sodium 935mg; Carbohydrate 25g (Dietary Fiber 1g, Sugars 13g); Protein 2g

% Daily Value: Vitamin A 8%; Vitamin C 12%; Calcium 4%; Iron 4%
Diet Exchanges: 1 Starch, 1 Vegetable, 1/2 Fat
Carbohydrate Choices: 1 1/2

Red Summer Soup

1 can (16 ounces) julienne beets, drained (reserve liquid)

1 small head red cabbage (about 1 pound), coarsely shredded

1 package (10 ounces) frozen raspberries in juice, undrained

1 tablespoon lemon juice

1 Heat 1 cup of water, beet liquid and cabbage to boiling in 3-quart saucepan; reduce heat. Cover and simmer 1 hour or until cabbage is very tender.

2 Carefully pour cabbage mixture and raspberries into work bowl of food processor fitted with steel blade or into blender container. Cover and process until smooth.

3 Return mixture to saucepan; stir in beets and lemon juice. Heat over medium heat, stirring occasionally until hot.

Betty's Tip 4 You

For a chilly change, **cover and refrigerate this soup for about 4 hours until it is completely chilled. Stir before serving and top each serving with a dollop of sour cream. Or use the chilled soup within a day or two.**

Nutrition Information

1 SERVING: Calories 60 (Calories from Fat 0); Fat 0g (Saturated 0g); Cholesterol 0mg; Sodium 120mg; Carbohydrate 13g (Dietary Fiber 5g, Sugars 10g); Protein 2g

% Daily Value: Vitamin A 0%; Vitamin C 42%; Calcium 4%; Iron 8%
Diet Exchanges: 1 Vegetable, 1/2 Fruit
Carbohydrate Choices: 1

Home-Style Potato Soup

1 can (14 1/2 ounces)
chicken broth

3 medium potatoes, cut into
large pieces (about 1 pound)

1 1/2 cups milk

2 medium green onions,
thinly sliced

1 Heat chicken broth and potatoes to boiling in 2-quart saucepan over high heat, stirring occasionally. Reduce heat; cover
and simmer about 15 minutes or until potatoes are tender.

2 Remove saucepan from heat, but do not drain. Break the
potatoes into smaller pieces with the potato masher or large
fork. The mixture should still be lumpy.

3 Stir the milk, 1/4 teaspoon salt, 1/8 teaspoon pepper and
green onions into the potato mixture. Heat over medium heat,
stirring occasionally until hot but do not boil to prevent
curdled appearance.

Betty's Tip
4 You

For a bit of variety, stir in 1/8 teaspoon dried
thyme leaves with the chicken broth and potatoes.
Or turn this soup into a tasty potato-cheese soup. When the
soup is hot, gradually stir in 1 1/2 cups shredded Cheddar
cheese until melted.

Nutrition Information

1 SERVING: Calories 120 (Calories from Fat 20); Fat 2g (Saturated 1g); Cholesterol 5mg; Sodium 530mg; Carbohydrate 19g (Dietary Fiber 1g, Sugars 4g); Protein 6g

% Daily Value: Vitamin A 4%; Vitamin C 6%; Calcium 10%; Iron 2%
Diet Exchanges: 1 Starch, 1/2 Milk
Carbohydrate Choices: 1

Home-Style Potato Soup

Vegetable Chowder in Bread Bowls

4 large hard rolls (about 3 1/2 inches in diameter)

2 cans (19 ounces each) ready-to-serve creamy potato soup with roasted garlic

1 bag (16 ounces) frozen potatoes, sweet peas and carrots

1 can (15 to 16 ounces) kidney beans, rinsed and drained

1 Cut thin, 2-inch round slice from top of rolls. Remove bread from inside of each roll, leaving 1/2-inch shell on side and bottom.

2 Heat soup, vegetables and beans in 3-quart saucepan over medium-high heat, stirring occasionally, 8 to 10 minutes, until vegetables are tender and soup is hot.

3 Fill soup bowls one-third full with soup. Place rolls on top of soup. Spoon additional soup into rolls, allowing some soup to overflow into bowls.

Betty's Tip 4 You

Here's a clever use for the bread that was removed from the inside of each roll—make bread crumbs. Place the bread in a food processor with 1 teaspoon of dried herbs such as thyme, oregano or parsley. Pulse until you have crumbs. You can also use these bread crumbs for the Ranch Chicken recipe on page 105.

Nutrition Information

1 SERVING: Calories 605 (Calories from Fat 180); Fat 20g (Saturated 5g); Cholesterol 25mg; Sodium 1650mg; Carbohydrate 94g (Dietary Fiber 13g, Sugars 6g); Protein 25g

% Daily Value: Vitamin A 100%; Vitamin C 12%; Calcium 12%; Iron 36%
Diet Exchanges: 6 Starch, 1 Lean Meat, 1 1/2 Fat
Carbohydrate Choices: 6

Vegetable Chowder in Bread Bowls

SUPER *Express*

Vegetable and Tortellini Soup

1 package (1.4 ounces) vegetable soup and recipe mix

1 package (9 ounces) refrigerated beef-filled tortellini

1 package (10 ounces) frozen chopped spinach, thawed and squeezed to drain

2 tablespoons grated Parmesan cheese

1 Mix 4 cups of water and soup mix in 3-quart saucepan. Heat to boiling, stirring occasionally; reduce heat to low.

2 Stir in tortellini and spinach. Simmer uncovered about 5 minutes, stirring occasionally, until tortellini is tender. Sprinkle each serving with about 1 teaspoon cheese.

Betty's Tip
4 You

Want a vegetarian version of this soup? **Substitute cheese-filled tortellini for the beef-filled.** Try different grated cheeses also, like pecarino romano for a sharper taste.

Nutrition Information

1 SERVING: Calories 125 (Calories from Fat 25); Fat 3g (Saturated 1g); Cholesterol 40mg; Sodium 750mg; Carbohydrate 15g (Dietary Fiber 2g, Sugars 1g); Protein 9g

% Daily Value: Vitamin A 66%; Vitamin C 4%; Calcium 10%; Iron 8%
Diet Exchanges: 1 Starch, 1 Very Lean Meat
Carbohydrate Choices: 1

German Potato Salad with Brats

1 tablespoon vegetable oil

6 fully cooked bratwurst
(1 to 1 1/2 pounds)

1 package (4.9 ounces) scalloped
potatoes in creamy seasoned sauce

2 to 3 tablespoons white vinegar

1 Heat oil in 10-inch skillet over medium heat. Cook bratwurst in oil, turning occasionally until brown; remove from skillet and drain.

2 Heat potatoes, Sauce Mix from potato mix and 2 3/4 cups of hot water to boiling in same skillet over high heat, stirring occasionally. Reduce heat; cover and simmer about 20 minutes, stirring occasionally, until potatoes are tender.

3 Stir in vinegar. Place bratwurst on potatoes. Cover and simmer about 3 minutes longer until bratwurst are hot.

Betty's Tip 4 You

It's **Oktoberfest anytime** with this quick and easy German potato salad made hearty with fully cooked bratwurst. Sprinkle with paprika for added color.

Nutrition Information

1 SERVING: Calories 435 (Calories from Fat 270); Fat 30g (Saturated 10g); Cholesterol 50mg; Sodium 1180mg; Carbohydrate 27g (Dietary Fiber 2g, Sugars 6g); Protein 14g

% Daily Value: Vitamin A 10%; Vitamin C 6%; Calcium 10%; Iron 6%
Diet Exchanges: 2 Starch, 1 High-Fat Meat, 4 Fat
Carbohydrate Choices: 2

Florentine Salad

1 1/2 pounds fresh spinach or 6 bunches leaf lettuce, coarsely shredded or torn into small pieces (4 1/2 quarts)

12 slices bacon, crisply cooked and crumbled

6 hard-cooked eggs, chopped

3/4 cup Catalina bottled salad dressing

1 Place spinach, bacon and eggs in extra-large salad bowl. Add dressing; gently toss until leaves are well coated.

2 Chill 1 hour before serving.

Betty's Tip 4 You

For an added flavor kick, **add 1 cup chopped green onions.**

Nutrition Information

1 SERVING: Calories 215 (Calories from Fat 145); Fat 16g (Saturated 4g); Cholesterol 165mg; Sodium 530mg; Carbohydrate 8g (Dietary Fiber 2g, Sugars 5); Protein 10g

% Daily Value: Vitamin A 100%; Vitamin C 16%; Calcium 8%; Iron 12%
Diet Exchanges: 1 Medium-Fat Meat, 2 Vegetable, 1 1/2 Fat
Carbohydrate Choices: 1/2

Quick BLT Salad

1 package (7.5 ounces) ranch and bacon pasta salad mix

1/2 cup mayonnaise or salad dressing

3 cups finely shredded lettuce

1 large tomato, coarsely chopped

1 Empty Pasta Mix into large pan 2/3 full of boiling water. Gently boil uncovered 15 minutes, stirring occasionally, until pasta is tender.

2 Drain pasta. Rinse with cold water. Shake to drain well.

3 Stir together Seasoning Mix from salad mix and mayonnaise in large bowl. Stir in pasta, lettuce and tomato until well blended. Serve immediately.

Betty's Tip 4 You

Get the great taste of the classic sandwich favorite in this quick and flavorful pasta salad. Add bacon flavor bits or chips for even more bacon taste.

Nutrition Information

1 SERVING: Calories 325 (Calories from Fat 155); Fat 17g (Saturated 2g); Cholesterol 11mg; Sodium 490mg; Carbohydrate 33g (Dietary Fiber 2g, Sugars 5g); Protein 8g

% Daily Value: Vitamin A 22%; Vitamin C 10%; Calcium 6%; Iron 8%
Diet Exchanges: 2 Starch, 1/2 High-Fat Meat, 1 Vegetable, 2 Fat
Carbohydrate Choices: 2

SUPER *Express*

Canadian Bacon and Gouda Salad

1 bag (10 ounces) washed fresh baby spinach

12 ounces sliced Canadian-style bacon, cut in half

8 ounces Gouda cheese, sliced

1/2 cup honey Dijon dressing

1 Divide spinach among 4 plates.

2 Top each serving with bacon and cheese. Drizzle with dressing.

Betty's Tip 4 You

Turn this salad into a sweet and savory meal by adding sliced peaches. Fresh peaches are always delicious, but if you can't find them, frozen or canned are tasty, too.

Nutrition Information

1 SERVING: Calories 450 (Calories from Fat 290); Fat 32g (Saturated 13g); Cholesterol 90mg; Sodium 1870mg; Carbohydrate 7g (Dietary Fiber 2g, Sugars 5g); Protein 33g

% Daily Value: Vitamin A 100%; Vitamin C 32%; Calcium 48%; Iron 14%
Diet Exchanges: 4 1/2 Medium-Fat Meat, 1 Vegetable, 2 Fat
Carbohydrate Choices: 1/2

Ham and Slaw Salad

SUPER
Express

1 pint (2 cups) deli coleslaw
(creamy style)

2 cans (8 ounces each) tropical
fruit salad, chilled and drained

1/2 cup golden raisins

1 1/2 cups cubed fully cooked
fat-free ham

1 If coleslaw is very wet, drain off excess liquid. Mix coleslaw,
fruit salad and raisins in large bowl.

2 Spoon coleslaw mixture into center of each of 4 plates. Make
indentation in center of each mound of coleslaw mixture;
fill with ham.

*Betty's Tip
4 You*

This salad is so easy it almost makes itself! **For
extra color and crunch, line the plates with crisp
lettuce leaves. Stir the ham, fruit and raisins into the coleslaw
and spoon onto the leaves.**

Nutrition Information

1 SERVING: Calories 395 (Calories from Fat 200); Fat 22g
(Saturated 4g); Cholesterol 40mg; Sodium 760mg;
Carbohydrate 36g (Dietary Fiber 3g, Sugars 27g); Protein 13g

% Daily Value: Vitamin A 58%; Vitamin C 38%; Calcium 6%; Iron 10%
Diet Exchanges: 1 Very Lean Meat, 2 1/2 Vegetable, 1 1/2 Fruit, 4 1/2 Fat
Carbohydrate Choices: 3 1/2

Warm Hot Dog Pasta Salad

1 package (7.75 ounces) classic pasta salad mix

1 package (1 pound) hot dogs

2 tablespoons vegetable oil

4 ounces process cheese spread loaf, shredded (1 cup)

1 Empty Pasta Mix into large pan 2/3 full of boiling water. Gently boil uncovered 20 minutes, stirring occasionally, until pasta is tender..

2 While pasta is cooking, heat hot dogs according to package directions. Slice into 1/2-inch pieces.

3 Drain pasta; rinse with cool water. Shake to drain well. Stir together Seasoning Mix from salad mix, 3 tablespoons cold water and oil in large bowl; stir in pasta, hot dogs and cheese. Serve immediately.

Betty's Tip 4 You

Got leftovers of this kid-friendly salad? Refrigerate and serve cold, right from the fridge. Add crisp carrot and celery sticks along with some apple wedges and you have a quick and easy lunch.

Nutrition Information

1 SERVING: Calories 480 (Calories from Fat 290); Fat 32g (Saturated 12g); Cholesterol 55mg; Sodium 1860mg; Carbohydrate 32g (Dietary Fiber 2g, Sugars 8g); Protein 16g

% Daily Value: Vitamin A 2%; Vitamin C 0%; Calcium 14%; Iron 10%
Diet Exchanges: 2 Starch, 1 1/2 High-Fat Meat, 4 Fat
Carbohydrate Choices: 2

Zesty Pasta Sausage Salad

1 package (8.1 ounces) roasted garlic Parmesan pasta salad mix

12 ounces spicy Italian sausage links

3 tablespoons vegetable oil

1 1/2 cups frozen French-style green beans, thawed and drained

1 Empty Pasta Mix into large pan 2/3 full of boiling water. Gently boil uncovered 12 minutes, stirring occasionally.

2 While pasta is cooking, cut sausages into 3/4-inch slices. Cook in 10-inch skillet over medium heat, stirring occasionally, until sausage is no longer pink; drain.

3 Drain pasta; rinse with cool water. Shake to drain well. Stir together Seasoning Mix from salad mix, 1/4 cup of cold water and oil in large bowl; stir in pasta, sausage and beans. Just before serving, toss with Topping from salad mix. Serve immediately, or refrigerate.

Betty's Tip 4 You

This is a little pasta salad that's big on flavor! Spicy sausage, pasta, green beans and a hint of garlic make this simple salad a meal to remember. Add garden-fresh flavor and punch up the color with chopped tomato or red bell pepper strips.

Nutrition Information

1 SERVING: Calories 470 (Calories from Fat 250); Fat 28g (Saturated 7g); Cholesterol 50mg; Sodium 1260mg; Carbohydrate 35g (Dietary Fiber 2g, Sugars 5g); Protein 19g

% Daily Value: Vitamin A 14%; Vitamin C 4%; Calcium 6%; Iron 12%
Diet Exchanges: 2 Starch, 1 1/2 High-Fat Meat, 1 Vegetable, 3 Fat
Carbohydrate Choices: 2

⏱ SUPER *Express*

Chicken Salad

1/2 cup mayonnaise or salad dressing

1 1/2 cups chopped cooked chicken or turkey

1 medium stalk celery, chopped (1/2 cup)

1 small onion, finely chopped (1/4 cup)

1 Stir 1/4 teaspoon salt and 1/4 teaspoon pepper into mayonnaise in medium bowl.

2 Add remaining ingredients; toss until evenly coated.

Betty's Tip
4 You

Classic chicken salad is also wonderful all by itself served on a lettuce-lined plate with some cut-up fresh vegetables or fruits. It is also delicious as a sandwich filling or to stuff a tomato. Or spoon it on an avocado half or slices of fresh pineapples.

Nutrition Information

1 SERVING: Calories 600 (Calories from Fat 460); Fat 51g (Saturated 9g); Cholesterol 125mg; Sodium 710mg; Carbohydrate 5g (Dietary Fiber 1g, Sugars 3g); Protein 30g

% Daily Value: Vitamin A 2%; Vitamin C 6%; Calcium 4%; Iron 8%
Diet Exchanges: 4 High-Fat Meat, 1 Vegetable, 4 Fat
Carbohydrate Choices: 0

Chicken Salad

Tuna-Vegetable Salad

1 can (12 ounces) tuna, drained

1 package (14 ounces) frozen precooked salad tortellini, rinsed and drained

1 bag (1 pound) frozen broccoli, cauliflower and carrots, thawed (or other combination)

1/2 cup creamy Parmesan or cucumber dressing

1 Place tuna, tortellini and vegetables in large bowl.

2 Add dressing; toss gently until evenly coated with dressing.

Betty's Tip 4 You

Have leftover chicken or salmon from the grill? **Toss it into this salad for a delicious treat. Try using a variation of frozen vegetables for a change such as with snow peas and water chestnuts.**

Nutrition Information

1 SERVING: Calories 300 (Calories from Fat 145); Fat 16g (Saturated 4g); Cholesterol 70mg; Sodium 390mg; Carbohydrate 18g (Dietary Fiber 3g, Sugars 4g); Protein 21g

% Daily Value: Vitamin A 48%; Vitamin C 42%; Calcium 8%; Iron 12%
Diet Exchanges: 1 Starch, 2 Lean Meat, 1 Vegetable, 2 Fat
Carbohydrate Choices: 1

Warm Bean and Spinach Salad

SUPER
Express

1 bag (10 ounces) washed fresh spinach

1 can (15 to 16 ounces) cannellini beans, rinsed and drained

1 large red bell pepper, coarsely chopped (1 1/2 cups)

2/3 cup Italian dressing

1 Remove large stems from spinach; tear spinach into bite-size pieces. Place spinach in large bowl. Add beans; set aside.

2 Heat bell pepper, dressing and 1/4 teaspoon pepper to boiling in 1-quart saucepan; reduce heat to low. Cook uncovered 2 minutes, stirring occasionally.

3 Pour bell pepper mixture over spinach and beans; toss. Serve warm.

Betty's Tip 4 You

This Italian salad bursts with flavor, color and texture. Try it when you want the lightness of a salad combined with the heartiness of a main dish. For a delicious change, use other beans, such as kidney beans, navy beans or chickpeas.

Nutrition Information

1 SERVING: Calories 335 (Calories from Fat 155); Fat 17g (Saturated 1g); Cholesterol 5mg; Sodium 20mg; Carbohydrate 36g (Dietary Fiber 9g, Sugars 7g); Protein 14g

% Daily Value: Vitamin A 100%; Vitamin C 100%; Calcium 20%; Iron 34%
Diet Exchanges: 2 Starch, 1 1/2 Lean Meat, 1 Vegetable, 1 1/2 Fat
Carbohydrate Choices: 2 1/2

4 Star Ideas

Pastabilities

Do you have some leftover cooked pasta? Turn it into a tasty pasta salad with these additions:

★ Add canned corn, diced bell peppers and salsa

★ Add cut-up cooked chicken, sun-dried tomatoes and prepared pesto

★ Add strips of salami, provolone cheese and bottled Caesar dressing

★ Add canned beans, green beans and Italian dressing

4 Star Ideas

Rice to the Rescue

Make leftover cooked rice the star of your meal with these quick fixes:

★ Turn 2 cups of leftover rice into fried rice by frying it with 2 beaten eggs, chopped frozen vegetables and soy sauce

★ Toss wild rice with dried cranberries, chopped walnuts and a sprinkling of sugar

★ Stir-fry rice with bite-size pieces of cooked pork sausage, chopped bell pepper and a can of tomato sauce

★ Or make it dessert—heat it up in a saucepan with milk, raisins and sugar for yummy rice pudding

2 Pronto Pastas and Grains

Cheesy Pasta, Veggies and Beef   36

One-Pan Pasta and Meatballs   38

🕐 Southwestern Skillet Stroganoff   40

🕐 Sausage with Fettuccine   41

🕐 Spaghetti Carbonara   42

🕐 Greek Lamb and Orzo   43

🕐 Garden Chicken and Fettuccine   44

Garden Vegetables, Chicken and Pasta Salad   46

🕐 Bow-Ties with Turkey, Pesto and Roasted Red Peppers   48

🕐 Chicken Tortellini with Portabella Mushroom Sauce   50

🕐 Angel Hair Pasta in Garlic Sauce   51

Alfredo Salmon and Noodles   52

🕐 Capellini with Lemon and Basil   54

Penne with Tomato and Smoked Cheese   55

🕐 Ravioli with Peppers and Sun-Dried Tomatoes   56

🕐 Quick Beef Tips and Vegetables   57

Savory Chicken and Rice   58

Dried Cherries and Turkey Rice Pilaf   59

Sautéed Polenta   60

🕐 Vegetable-Rice Skillet   61

Photos: opposite top: Bow-Ties with Turkey, Pesto and Roasted Red Peppers (page 48); opposite bottom: One-Pan Pasta and Meatballs (page 38)

🕐 **SUPER**Express *ready in 20 minutes or less*

Cheesy Pasta, Veggies and Beef

1 pound ground beef

1 bag (1 pound) frozen pasta, broccoli, corn and carrots in garlic-seasoned sauce (or other combination)

1 can (10 ounces) condensed Cheddar cheese soup

Cheese-flavored topping or cheese-flavored tiny fish-shaped crackers

1 Cook beef in 10-inch skillet over medium heat 8 to 10 minutes, stirring occasionally, until brown; drain.

2 Stir pasta mixture, soup and 1 cup of water into beef. Heat to boiling; reduce heat. Cover and simmer 5 to 7 minutes, stirring occasionally, until vegetables are tender. Sprinkle with cheese topping.

Betty's Tip 4 You

Serve this super-easy skillet meal with a salad of crisp greens and cherry tomatoes and fresh fruit like green grapes and sherbet or sorbet for dessert.

Nutrition Information

1 SERVING: Calories 490 (Calories from Fat 270); Fat 30g (Saturated 13g); Cholesterol 85mg; Sodium 1180mg; Carbohydrate 36g (Dietary Fiber 3g, Sugars 7g); Protein 29g

% Daily Value: Vitamin A 56%; Vitamin C 16%; Calcium 10%; Iron 18%
Diet Exchanges: 2 Starch, 3 Medium-Fat Meat, 1 Vegetable, 2 Fat
Carbohydrate Choices: 2 1/2

Cheesy Pasta, Veggies and Beef

One-Pan Pasta and Meatballs

1 jar (26 to 28 ounces) tomato pasta sauce (any variety)

1 1/2 cups uncooked elbow macaroni pasta (4 1/2 ounces)

20 frozen fully cooked Italian-flavor or regular meatballs, 1 inch in diameter (from 18-ounce bag)

1 can (2 1/4 ounces) sliced ripe olives, drained

1 Heat 1 cup of water and pasta sauce to boiling in 10-inch skillet. Stir in pasta, meatballs and olives. Heat to boiling; reduce heat to medium.

2 Cover and cook 15 to 20 minutes, stirring occasionally, until pasta is tender.

Betty's Tip 4 You

Don't have ripe olives on hand? **Use 1 small green bell pepper, cut into 1/2-inch pieces, or a 6-ounce jar of sliced mushrooms, drained, instead.** For added appetite appeal sprinkle with shredded Parmesan or mozzarella cheese.

Nutrition Information
1 SERVING: Calories 520 (Calories from Fat 180); Fat 20g (Saturated 6g); Cholesterol 70mg; Sodium 1450mg; Carbohydrate 68g (Dietary Fiber 5g, Sugars 16g); Protein 22g

% Daily Value: Vitamin A 26%; Vitamin C 22%; Calcium 10%; Iron 26%
Diet Exchanges: 5 Starch, 1 Medium-Fat Meat, 1 Fat
Carbohydrate Choices: 4 1/2

One-Pan Pasta and Meatballs

SUPER *Express*

Southwestern Skillet Stroganoff

1 pound ground beef

1 jar (16 ounces) thick-and-chunky salsa

2 cups uncooked wagon wheel pasta (6 ounces)

1/2 cup sour cream

1 Cook beef in 10-inch skillet over medium-high heat, stirring occasionally, until brown; drain. Stir in 1 cup of water, salsa, pasta and 1/2 teaspoon of salt. Heat to boiling; reduce heat to low.

2 Cover and simmer about 10 minutes, stirring occasionally, until pasta is tender. Stir in sour cream; cook just until hot.

Betty's Tip 4 You

Top off this family-pleasing pasta skillet supper with crushed corn chips or flavored tortilla chips and chopped fresh cilantro. Serve with cooked green beans to round out the meal.

Nutrition Information

1 SERVING: Calories 485 (Calories from Fat 205); Fat 23g (Saturated 10g); Cholesterol 85mg; Sodium 580mg; Carbohydrate 41g (Dietary Fiber 3g, Sugars 6g); Protein 29g

% Daily Value: Vitamin A 20%; Vitamin C 12%; Calcium 8%; Iron 24%
Diet Exchanges: 3 Starch, 3 Medium-Fat Meat, 1/2 Fat
Carbohydrate Choices: 3

Sausage with Fettuccine

1 package (9 ounces) refrigerated
fettuccine

2 cans (15 ounces each) chunky
garlic-and-herb tomato sauce

1 bag (1 pound) frozen stir-fry
bell peppers and onions, thawed

1 ring (1 pound) fully cooked
95% fat-free turkey kielbasa
sausage, cut into 1/2-inch pieces

1 Cook and drain fettuccine as directed on package; keep warm.

2 Heat tomato sauce, pepper mixture and sausage to boiling in same saucepan. Stir in fettuccine; heat through.

**Betty's Tip
4 You**

Have fun with your fettuccine—try spinach fettuccine in this hearty dish. And try different sausages like chorizo or pepperoni slices.

Nutrition Information

1 SERVING: Calories 610 (Calories from Fat 135); Fat 15g (Saturated 4g); Cholesterol 110mg; Sodium 2200mg; Carbohydrate 90g (Dietary Fiber 6g, Sugars 19g); Protein 29g

% Daily Value: Vitamin A 32%; Vitamin C 70%; Calcium 8%; Iron 30%
Diet Exchanges: 5 1/2 Starch, 2 Medium-Fat Meat, 1 Vegetable
Carbohydrate Choices: 6

SUPER *Express*

Spaghetti Carbonara

1 package (16 ounces) spaghetti

6 slices bacon, cut into 1/2-inch squares

1 cup grated Parmesan cheese

3/4 cup fat-free cholesterol-free egg product

1 Cook spaghetti in Dutch oven as directed on package. Cook bacon in 10-inch skillet over medium heat, stirring occasionally, until almost crisp.

2 Drain spaghetti; return to Dutch oven. Add bacon, bacon fat and 1/2 cup of the cheese to spaghetti; toss over low heat. Stir in egg product. Cook over low heat 2 minutes, tossing mixture constantly, until egg product coats spaghetti; remove from heat. Sprinkle with remaining 1/2 cup cheese. Serve immediately.

Betty's Tip 4 You

The original recipe used fresh eggs. **Because this dish doesn't cook very long the eggs aren't fully cooked.** However, today to ensure food safety, we call for fat-free egg product which doesn't require long cooking to be safe. You will find these egg products in the dairy or freezer case.

Nutrition Information
1 SERVING: Calories 425 (Calories from Fat 90); Fat 10g (Saturated 4g); Cholesterol 20mg; Sodium 50mg; Carbohydrate 62g (Dietary Fiber 3g, Sugars 3g); Protein 22g

% Daily Value: Vitamin A 6%; Vitamin C 0%; Calcium 26%; Iron 20%
Diet Exchanges: 4 Starch, 1 1/2 Medium-Fat Meat
Carbohydrate Choices: 4

Greek Lamb and Orzo

1 pound ground lamb or beef

2 cans (16 ounces each) stewed tomatoes, undrained

1 cup uncooked orzo or rosamarina pasta (6 ounces)

1/4 cup plain yogurt

1 Cook lamb in 10-inch skillet over medium-high heat, stirring occasionally, until no longer pink; drain. Stir in stewed tomatoes, orzo, 1/4 teaspoon of salt and 1/4 teaspoon of pepper. Heat to boiling; reduce heat to low.

2 Cover and simmer about 12 minutes, stirring frequently, until tomato liquid is absorbed and orzo is tender. Serve with yogurt.

Betty's Tip
4 You

Plain yogurt tops off this dish perfectly. You may want to have a little extra on hand and dip slices of warm pita bread into the yogurt as a delicious side. Add a sliced cucumber and tomato salad sprinkled with feta cheese for an easy Greek dinner.

Nutrition Information

1 SERVING: Calories 420 (Calories from Fat 155); Fat 17g (Saturated 7g); Cholesterol 75mg; Sodium 690mg; Carbohydrate 43g (Dietary Fiber 3g, Sugars 13g); Protein 24g

% Daily Value: Vitamin A 10%; Vitamin C 22%; Calcium 10%; Iron 20%
Diet Exchanges: 2 Starch, 2 Medium-Fat Meat, 2 Vegetable, 1 Fat
Carbohydrate Choices: 3

SUPER
Express

Garden Chicken and Fettuccine

8 ounces uncooked fettuccine

3 cups chopped cooked chicken
or turkey

3 tablespoons olive or vegetable oil

2 large tomatoes, chopped (2 cups)

1 Cook and drain pasta as directed on package; return to saucepan.

2 Add chicken, oil, tomatoes and 1 teaspoon salt to pasta; toss until evenly coated.

Betty's Tip
4 You

For extra flavor and a pretty presentation, **top** this already flavor-packed pasta with chopped fresh basil leaves.

Nutrition Information

1 SERVING: Calories 325 (Calories from Fat 115); Fat 13g (Saturated 3g); Cholesterol 90mg; Sodium 460mg; Carbohydrate 27g (Dietary Fiber 2g, Sugars 2g); Protein 25g

% Daily Value: Vitamin A 10%; Vitamin C 8%; Calcium 2%; Iron 14%
Diet Exchanges: 1 1/2 Starch, 3 Lean Meat, 1 Vegetable
Carbohydrate Choices: 2

Garden Chicken and Fettuccine

Garden Vegetables, Chicken and Pasta Salad

1 bag (1 pound) frozen primavera vegetables with pasta (or other combination)

1 cup shredded cooked chicken or turkey

2 medium stalks celery, sliced (1 cup)

1/4 cup ranch dressing

1 Cook vegetables as directed on package.

2 Add chicken, celery and dressing; toss until evenly coated. Cover and refrigerate 10 minutes to cool.

Betty's Tip
4 You

Want a twist on this main dish? Try using frozen creamy Cheddar vegetables with pasta or herb-seasoned vegetables with pasta.

Nutrition Information
1 SERVING: Calories 305 (Calories from Fat 135); Fat 15g (Saturated 3g); Cholesterol 40mg; Sodium 480mg; Carbohydrate 25g (Dietary Fiber 3g, Sugars 5g); Protein 18g

% Daily Value: Vitamin A 18%; Vitamin C 12%; Calcium 12%; Iron 8%
Diet Exchanges: 1 1/2 Starch, 2 Medium-Fat Meat, 1 Fat
Carbohydrate Choices: 1 1/2

Garden Vegetables, Chicken and Pasta Salad

SUPER *Express*

Bow-Ties with Turkey, Pesto and Roasted Red Peppers

3 cups uncooked farfalle (bow-tie) pasta (6 ounces)

2 cups cubed cooked turkey breast or chicken

1/2 cup basil pesto

1/2 cup coarsely chopped roasted red bell peppers (from 7-ounce jar)

1 Cook pasta in 3-quart saucepan as directed on package; drain. Return pasta to saucepan.

2 Add turkey, pesto and bell peppers to pasta. Heat over low heat, stirring constantly, until hot.

Betty's Tip 4 You

Make the meal complete by serving with a loaf of Italian bread and extra-virgin olive oil for dipping. If you like olives, add some sliced olives with the turkey. Serve with slices of tomatoes.

Nutrition Information

1 SERVING: Calories 420 (Calories from Fat 160); Fat 18g (Saturated 4g); Cholesterol 65mg; Sodium 310mg; Carbohydrate 36g (Dietary Fiber 3g, Sugars 3); Protein 29g

% Daily Value: Vitamin A 30%; Vitamin C 34%; Calcium 14%; Iron 20%
Diet Exchanges: 2 1/2 Starch, 3 Lean Meat, 1 Fat
Carbohydrate Choices: 2 1/2

Bow-Ties with Turkey, Pesto and Roasted Red Peppers

SUPER
Express

Chicken Tortellini with Portabella Mushroom Sauce

2 packages (9 ounces each) refrigerated chicken-filled tortellini pasta

1 tablespoon margarine or butter

3 cups chopped portabella or shiitake mushrooms (6 ounces)

1 container (10 ounces) refrigerated Alfredo sauce

1 Cook and drain tortellini as directed on package.

2 While pasta is cooking, heat margarine in 10-inch skillet over medium heat. Cook mushrooms in margarine, stirring occasionally, until brown and tender. Add Alfredo sauce and tortellini. Gently stir until pasta is evenly coated.

Betty's Tip
4 You

The flavors in this appealing main dish **will explode by adding 2 teaspoons chopped fresh sage, basil or thyme.**

Nutrition Information

1 SERVING: Calories 370 (Calories from Fat 205); Fat 23g (Saturated 12g); Cholesterol 125mg; Sodium 650mg; Carbohydrate 24g (Dietary Fiber 1g, Sugars 1g); Protein 17g

% Daily Value: Vitamin A 16%; Vitamin C 0%; Calcium 18%; Iron 10%
Diet Exchanges: 1 1/2 Starch, 2 Medium-Fat Meat, 2 Fat
Carbohydrate Choices: 1 1/2

Angel Hair Pasta in Garlic Sauce

1 package (16 ounces) capellini (angel hair) pasta

1/4 cup olive or vegetable oil

1/4 cup chopped fresh parsley

4 cloves garlic, finely chopped

1 Cook and drain pasta as directed on package.

2 While pasta is cooking, heat oil in 12-inch skillet over medium heat. Cook parsley and garlic in oil about 3 minutes, stirring frequently, until garlic is soft.

3 Add pasta to mixture in skillet; toss gently until pasta is evenly coated.

Betty's Tip
4 You

Sprinkle the dish with 1/2 cup freshly grated or shredded Parmesan cheese for extra spark of flavor. Pressed for time? Use 2 teaspoons of jarred chopped garlic for the garlic cloves.

Nutrition Information

1 SERVING: Calories 375 (Calories from Fat 90); Fat 10g (Saturated 1g); Cholesterol 0mg; Sodium 5mg; Carbohydrate 61g (Dietary Fiber 3g, Sugars 3g); Protein 10g

% Daily Value: Vitamin A 4%; Vitamin C 2%; Calcium 2%; Iron 18%
Diet Exchanges: 4 Starch, 1 Fat
Carbohydrate Choices: 4

Alfredo Salmon and Noodles

3 cups uncooked wide egg noodles (6 ounces)

1 package (10 ounces) frozen chopped broccoli

1/2 cup Alfredo sauce

1 can (6 ounces) skinless boneless pink salmon, drained and flaked

1 Cook noodles as directed on package, adding broccoli for the last 4 to 5 minutes of cooking. Drain and return to saucepan.

2 Stir in remaining ingredients with 1/8 teaspoon of pepper. Cook over low heat 4 to 6 minutes, stirring occasionally, until hot.

Betty's Tip 4 You

Continue with the flavors of Italy by adding 1/3 cup of pesto with sun-dried tomatoes with the remaining ingredients. Don't have salmon? Use a 6-ounce can of water-packed tuna, drained, instead.

Nutrition Information

1 SERVING: Calories 330 (Calories from Fat 125); Fat 14g (Saturated 7g); Cholesterol 90mg; Sodium 390mg; Carbohydrate 33g (Dietary Fiber 3g, Sugars 1g); Protein 18g

% Daily Value: Vitamin A 30%; Vitamin C 20%; Calcium 20%; Iron 14%
Diet Exchanges: 2 Starch, 1 1/2 Lean Meat, 1 Vegetable, 1 1/2 Fat
Carbohydrate Choices: 2

Alfredo Salmon and Noodles

SUPER *Express*

Capellini with Lemon and Basil

8 ounces uncooked capellini
(angel hair) pasta

1/4 cup chopped fresh basil leaves

1/4 cup lemon juice

3 tablespoons olive or vegetable oil

1 Cook and drain pasta as directed on package; return pasta to saucepan.

2 Add basil, lemon juice, olive oil and 1/2 teaspoon pepper; toss until pasta is evenly coated.

Betty's Tip
4 You

This fresh, light pasta not only makes a great light main dish but it also pairs well with grilled fish and chicken. If you'd like a more lemony taste, add 1 tablespoon grated lemon peel.

Nutrition Information

1 SERVING: Calories 265 (Calories from Fat 100); Fat 11g (Saturated 1g); Cholesterol 0mg; Sodium 5mg; Carbohydrate 35g (Dietary Fiber 2g, Sugars 2g); Protein 6g

% Daily Value: Vitamin A 4%; Vitamin C 2%; Calcium 0%; Iron 10%
Diet Exchanges: 2 Starch, 2 Fat
Carbohydrate Choices: 2

Penne with Tomato and Smoked Cheese

3 cups uncooked penne pasta
(9 ounces)

1 can (14 1/2 ounces) diced
tomatoes, undrained

2 cups Alfredo sauce

1 cup shredded smoked or regular
mozzarella cheese (4 ounces)

1 Heat oven to 350°. Grease 1 1/2-quart casserole. Cook and drain pasta as directed on package.

2 While pasta is cooking, heat tomatoes to boiling in 2-quart saucepan; reduce heat to medium. Cook uncovered 6 to 8 minutes, stirring occasionally, until liquid has evaporated.

3 Heat Alfredo sauce in 2-quart saucepan over medium-low heat; stir in cheese until melted.

4 Mix sauce, pasta and tomatoes. Pour into casserole. Bake uncovered about 30 minutes or until hot in center.

Betty's Tip 4 You

An incredibly quick and easy pasta dish of alfredo sauce, tomatoes and cheese. The sauce gives so much flavor for such a simple meal.

Nutrition Information

1 SERVING: Calories 500 (Calories from Fat 260); Fat 29g (Saturated 18g); Cholesterol 90mg; Sodium 540mg; Carbohydrate 42g (Dietary Fiber 2g, Sugars 4g); Protein 18g

% Daily Value: Vitamin A 24%; Vitamin C 8%; Calcium 36%; Iron 12%
Diet Exchanges: 3 Starch, 1 High-Fat Meat, 3 1/2 Fat
Carbohydrate Choices: 3

SUPER *Express*

Ravioli with Peppers and Sun-Dried Tomatoes

2 packages (9 ounces each) refrigerated Italian sausage–filled ravioli

1/2 cup julienne sun-dried tomatoes in oil and herbs, drained, and 2 tablespoons oil reserved

1 bag (1 pound) frozen stir-fry bell peppers and onions, thawed and drained

2 cups shredded Havarti or provolone cheese (8 ounces)

1 Cook and drain ravioli as directed on package.

2 Heat oil from tomatoes in 12-inch skillet over medium heat. Cook bell pepper mixture in oil 2 minutes, stirring occasionally. Stir in tomatoes and ravioli. Cook, stirring occasionally, until hot.

3 Sprinkle with cheese. Cover and cook 1 to 2 minutes or until cheese is melted.

Betty's Tip 4 You

For a fun, stringy cheese the kids will love—or if you'd like a milder flavor—use shredded mozzarella instead of Havarti or provolone.

Nutrition Information

1 SERVING: Calories 405 (Calories from Fat 225); Fat 25g (Saturated 11g); Cholesterol 135mg; Sodium 880mg; Carbohydrate 26g (Dietary Fiber 3g, Sugars 5g); Protein 19g

% Daily Value: Vitamin A 42%; Vitamin C 38%; Calcium 28%; Iron 14%
Diet Exchanges: 1 1/2 Starch, 2 Medium-Fat Meat, 1 1/2 Vegetable, 2 1/2 Fat • **Carbohydrate Choices:** 2

Quick Beef Tips and Vegetables

SUPER
Express

1/2-pound beef boneless sirloin tip steak

1 bag (1pound) frozen mixed vegetables with snap pea pods (or other combination)

1/4 cup stir-fry sauce with garlic and ginger

2 cups hot cooked rice

1 Remove fat from beef. Cut beef into 1/2-inch cubes.

2 Spray 12-inch nonstick skillet with cooking spray; heat over medium-high heat. Add beef; stir-fry about 2 minutes or until brown. Add vegetables and 1 tablespoon of water; stir-fry 1 minute.

3 Stir in stir-fry sauce until well mixed; reduce heat to medium. Cover and cook 5 to 7 minutes, stirring frequently, until vegetables are crisp-tender. Serve with rice.

Betty's Tip
4 You

When using frozen stir-fry vegetables, look for snap pea pods instead of snow (Chinese) pea pods. Snap pea pods retain their crispness through freezing and stir-frying.

Nutrition Information
1 SERVING: Calories 215 (Calories from Fat 20); Fat 2g (Saturated 1g); Cholesterol 30mg; Sodium 920mg; Carbohydrate 32g (Dietary Fiber 3, Sugars 4g); Protein 17g

% Daily Value: Vitamin A 18%; Vitamin C 36%; Calcium 4%; Iron 20%
Diet Exchanges: 1 1/2 Starch, 1 1/2 Very Lean Meat, 1 1/2 Vegetable
Carbohydrate Choices: 2

Savory Chicken and Rice

4 boneless, skinless chicken breast halves (about 1 pound)

1 1/2 cups sliced mushrooms (4 ounces)

1 cup baby-cut carrots

1 package (4.1 ounces) long grain and wild rice mix with chicken and herbs

1 Remove fat from chicken. Cut chicken into 1-inch pieces.

2 Spray 10-inch nonstick skillet with cooking spray; heat over medium heat. Cook chicken in skillet about 5 minutes, stirring occasionally, until no longer pink in center. Stir in remaining ingredients with 1 1/2 cups of water.

3 Heat to boiling; reduce heat to low. Cover and simmer 15 minutes, stirring occasionally. Uncover and simmer about 3 minutes longer, stirring occasionally, until carrots are tender and liquid is absorbed.

Betty's Tip 4 You

Skinless chicken breast—loaded with vitamin B-6, niacin and zinc—is the leanest cut of chicken. Serving for serving, chicken breast has less fat than dark meat, but the amount of cholesterol is the same.

Nutrition Information

1 SERVING: Calories 280 (Calories from Fat 45); Fat 5g (Saturated 1g); Cholesterol 75mg; Sodium 440mg; Carbohydrate 28g (Dietary Fiber 2g, Sugars 3g); Protein 31g

% Daily Value: Vitamin A 100%; Vitamin C 2%; Calcium 2%; Iron 12%
Diet Exchanges: 2 Starch, 3 Very Lean Meat, 1/2 Fat
Carbohydrate Choices: 2

Dried Cherries and Turkey Rice Pilaf

1/2 pound ground turkey breast

4 medium green onions, sliced (1/4 cup)

1 package (6 3/4 ounces) fast-cooking long grain and wild rice mix seasoned with herbs

1/2 cup dried cherries

1 Spray 3-quart saucepan with cooking spray; heat over medium heat. Cook turkey and onions in saucepan about 8 minutes, stirring occasionally, until turkey is no longer pink. Stir in 2 cups of water and seasoning packet from rice mix. Heat to boiling, stirring occasionally; reduce heat to low.

2 Stir in rice and dried cherries. Cover and simmer about 5 minutes or until rice is tender.

Betty's Tip 4 You

Use your favorite dried fruits in this savory pilaf— add 1/2 cup golden raisins, dried cranberries, chopped dried peaches, or apricots for the cherries. Or try a combination of two dried fruits.

Nutrition Information

1 SERVING: Calories 250 (Calories from Fat 35); Fat 4g (Saturated 1g); Cholesterol 40mg; Sodium 400mg; Carbohydrate 37g (Dietary Fiber 2g, Sugars 12g); Protein 16g

% Daily Value: Vitamin A 2%; Vitamin C 4%; Calcium 2%; Iron 10%
Diet Exchanges: 2 1/2 Starch, 1 Lean Meat
Carbohydrate Choices: 2 1/2

Sautéed Polenta

1 cup whole kernel corn

1 teaspoon margarine or butter

1 cup cornmeal

1 Spray rectangular baking dish, 11 × 7 × 1 1/2 inches, with cooking spray. Heat 4 cups of water, whole kernel corn, margarine, 1/2 teaspoon salt and 1/4 teaspoon pepper to boiling in 2-quart saucepan.

2 Gradually add cornmeal, stirring constantly; reduce heat to medium-low. Cook 8 to 12 minutes, stirring occasionally, until mixture pulls away from the side of saucepan. Pour into baking dish. Cool 15 minutes. Cover and refrigerate about 1 hour or until firm.

3 Heat oven to 250°. Cut polenta into 8 pieces. Spray 10-inch nonstick skillet with cooking spray; heat over medium heat. Cook 4 pieces polenta at a time in skillet about 5 minutes on each side or until light brown. Place on ungreased cookie sheet; keep warm in oven while cooking remaining pieces.

Betty's Tip 4 You

Top with your favorite spaghetti sauce and a generous sprinkle of shredded cheese. Or for a lighter meal, serve with salsa, sour cream and sliced olives.

Nutrition Information
1 SERVING: Calories 155 (Calories from Fat 20); Fat 2g (Saturated 0g); Cholesterol 0mg; Sodium 310mg; Carbohydrate 35g (Dietary Fiber 4g, Sugars 3g); Protein 4g

% Daily Value: Vitamin A 4%; Vitamin C 0%; Calcium 0%; Iron 8%
Diet Exchanges: 2 Starch
Carbohydrate Choices: 2

Vegetable-Rice Skillet

1 can (14 1/2 ounces) vegetable broth

2 tablespoons margarine or butter

1 bag (1 pound) frozen cauliflower, carrots and asparagus (or other combination)

1 package (6.2 ounces) fast-cooking long-grain and wild rice mix

1 Heat broth and margarine to boiling in 10-inch skillet. Stir in vegetables, rice and seasoning packet from rice mix. Heat to boiling; reduce heat.

2 Cover and simmer 5 to 6 minutes or until vegetables and rice are tender.

Betty's Tip 4 You

Add cheese appeal to this skillet meal by garnishing with 3/4 cup shredded Cheddar cheese, shredded mozzarella or a combination of both.

Nutrition Information

1 SERVING: Calories 480 (Calories from Fat 70); Fat 8g (Saturated 2g); Cholesterol 0mg; Sodium 550mg; Carbohydrate 97g (Dietary Fiber 5g, Sugars 3g); Protein 10g

% Daily Value: Vitamin A 74%; Vitamin C 6%; Calcium 4%; Iron 18%
Diet Exchanges: 6 Starch, 1 Vegetable
Carbohydrate Choices: 6 1/2

4 Star Ideas

Personalized Pizza

Bring out a ready-to-serve pizza crust and make it your own by topping it with these great combos, then just pop it in a 400° oven for 10 to 15 minutes:

★ Hummus, sliced olives and chopped tomato

★ Chunky salsa, shredded Monterey Jack cheese and canned black beans

★ Cooked brown-and-serve pork sausage links, cut into pieces, scrambled eggs and shredded Cheddar cheese

★ Cream cheese, fresh fruit (such as strawberries, grapes or peaches) and a sprinkling of sugar

4 Star Ideas

Sandwich Savvy

Break out of your sandwich rut with these delicious ideas:

★ Bagel with honey mustard, sliced honey baked turkey and sliced Muenster cheese

★ Pumpernickel bread with sliced ham, sliced pears and cream cheese

★ Pastrami on a kaiser roll with creamy horseradish sauce and sliced tomato

★ Stuff pita bread with tuna salad from the deli, chopped apples and raisins

3

Sumptuous Sandwiches and Perfect Pizzas

🕐 Honey-Ham Bagel Sandwiches   64

Sizzling Sausage Hoagie   65

🕐 Pizza Dogs   66

Chicken Quesadillas   68

Hot Chicken Sub   70

🕐 Philly Turkey Panini   72

Honey-Mustard Chicken Sandwiches   74

🕐 Quick Chicken Barbecue Sandwiches   75

🕐 Broiled Bean Sandwiches   76

Caramelized-Onion Focaccia Wedges   77

Double-Decker Grilled Cheese Sandwiches   78

🕐 Italian Vegetable Focaccia Sandwich   80

🕐 Mozzarella and Tomato Melts   81

🕐 Peanut Butter and Banana Wraps   82

Vegetable Tortillas   83

Beef 'n Cheese Calzone   84

Ranchero Beef Pizza   85

🕐 BBQ Chicken Pizza   86

Pizza Monterey   88

🕐 Easy Bagel Pizzas   89

Photos: opposite top: BBQ Chicken Pizza (page 86); opposite bottom: Honey-Mustard Chicken Sandwiches (page 74)

🕐 **SUPER**Express *ready in 20 minutes or less*

SUPER *Express*

Honey-Ham Bagel Sandwiches

2 pumpernickel bagels,
split and toasted

4 teaspoons honey mustard

4 slices (1 ounce each) fully cooked
honey ham

4 thin slices (1/2 ounce each)
Swiss cheese

1 Heat oven to 400°.

2 Spread each bagel half with 1 teaspoon of mustard. Top each
with one slice of ham and a slice of cheese. Place on cookie
sheet. Bake 3 to 5 minutes or until cheese is melted.

Betty's Tip
4 You

Want to make your own honey mustard? Mix
equal parts of honey and mustard. Feel free to vary
the types of mustard and honey you use, to make great
new combinations.

Nutrition Information
1 SANDWICH: Calories 200 (Calories from Fat 65); Fat 7g
(Saturated 3g); Cholesterol 30mg; Sodium 580mg;
Carbohydrate 21g (Dietary Fiber 1g, Sugars 5); Protein 13g

% Daily Value: Vitamin A 2%; Vitamin C 0%; Calcium 14%; Iron 6%
Diet Exchanges: 1 1/2 Starch, 1 1/2 Lean Meat
Carbohydrate Choices: 1 1/2

Sizzling Sausage Hoagie

6 fully cooked sausages or hot dogs

1 large green bell pepper,
cut into 6 strips

About 3/4 cups Italian dressing

1 loaf (1 pound) unsliced French
bread, cut horizontally in half

1 Spray grill rack with cooking spray. Heat coals or gas grill for direct heat.

2 Thread whole sausages and bell pepper strips crosswise alternately on one 14-inch flat metal skewer. Brush dressing on cut sides of bread.

3 Grill sausages and pepper strips uncovered about 6 inches from medium heat 8 to 12 minutes, turning and brushing frequently with dressing, until brown. Add bread, cut sides down, for last 3 to 4 minutes of grilling until golden brown.

4 To serve, place skewer of sausages and pepper strips on bottom half of bread. Top with top of bread; pull out skewer. Cut bread crosswise into 6 servings.

Betty's Tip 4 You

A flat-bladed skewer works best for this recipe, as the sausage and bell pepper won't spin on the skewer when you turn it. If you don't have a flat-bladed skewer, thread sausages and peppers on two round-bladed skewers and place them side-by-side on the grill.

Nutrition Information

1 SANDWICH: Calories 535 (Calories from Fat 295); Fat 33g (Saturated 8g); Cholesterol 45mg; Sodium 1360mg; Carbohydrate 43g (Dietary Fiber 3g,Sugars 4g); Protein 16g

% Daily Value: Vitamin A 2%; Vitamin C 20%; Calcium 10%; Iron 16%
Diet Exchanges: 3 Starch, 1 High-Fat Meat, 4 1/2 Fat
Carbohydrate Choices: 3

SUPER Express

Pizza Dogs

1/2 cup pizza sauce

8 hot dogs

8 hot dog buns, split

1 cup shredded mozzarella cheese
(4 ounces)

1 Pour pizza sauce into microwavable bowl. Cover bowl with waxed paper. Microwave on High 30 to 45 seconds or until hot; keep warm.

2 Place 4 hot dogs on microwavable plate lined with paper towel. Pierce several times with fork. Cover with paper towel. Microwave on High 1 minute 10 seconds to 1 minute 30 seconds until hot. Let stand 3 minutes. Repeat with remaining hot dogs. Serve on buns. Top with pizza sauce and cheese.

Betty's Tip 4 You

You can also grill the hot dogs, cook them on a griddle or in a skillet if you like your hot dogs browned.

Nutrition Information
1 SANDWICH: Calories 315 (Calories from Fat 160); Fat 18g (Saturated 7g); Cholesterol 35mg; Sodium 910mg; Carbohydrate 25g (Dietary Fiber 1g, Sugars 7g); Protein 13g

% Daily Value: Vitamin A 4%; Vitamin C 2%; Calcium 18%; Iron 10%
Diet Exchanges: 1 1/2 Starch, 1 1/2 High-Fat Meat, 1 Fat
Carbohydrate Choices: 1 1/2

Pizza Dogs

Chicken Quesadillas

10 tomato-flavor or plain flour tortillas (6 to 8 inches in diameter)

2 cups shredded Monterey Jack cheese (8 ounces)

1 cup chopped cooked chicken

1 container (6 ounces) frozen guacamole, thawed

1 Spray one side of each tortilla with cooking spray. Place 5 of the tortillas, sprayed sides down, on cutting board. Sprinkle with cheese and chicken. Top with remaining tortillas, sprayed sides up.

2 Put 1 quesadilla in 10-inch skillet or on griddle. Cook over medium-high heat 2 minutes; turn. Cook about 2 minutes longer or until bottom tortilla is light golden brown and cheese is melted. Repeat with remaining quesadillas.

3 Cut quesadillas into wedges. Serve with guacamole.

Betty's Tip
4 You

Looking for the easy way out? Assemble the quesadillas on a cookie sheet, and bake them in a 350° oven for 5 to 7 minutes.

Nutrition Information

1 SERVING: Calories 410 (Calories from Fat 200); Fat 22g (Saturated 10g); Cholesterol 65mg; Sodium 650mg; Carbohydrate 30g (Dietary Fiber 3g, Sugars 2g); Protein 23g

% Daily Value: Vitamin A 12%; Vitamin C 6%; Calcium 38%; Iron 12%
Diet Exchanges: 2 Starch, 2 1/2 High-Fat Meat
Carbohydrate Choices: 3

Chicken Quesadillas

Hot Chicken Sub

6 frozen breaded chicken breast patties

1 loaf (1 pound) French bread, cut horizontally in half

1/2 cup creamy Italian dressing

1 Prepare chicken as directed on package.

2 Spread cut sides of bread with dressing. Layer hot chicken patties on bottom half of bread. Top with remaining half of bread. Cut into 6 pieces.

Betty's Tip
4 You

Dress up this sandwich **with lettuce and tomato** slices. For extra crunch add thin slices of cucumber or bell pepper rings.

Nutrition Information
1 SERVING: Calories 530 (Calories from Fat 235); Fat 26g (Saturated 5g); Cholesterol 50mg; Sodium 1180mg; Carbohydrate 51g (Dietary Fiber 2g, Sugars 3g); Protein 23g

% Daily Value: Vitamin A 0%; Vitamin C 0%; Calcium 8%; Iron 20%
Diet Exchanges: 3 1/2 Starch, 2 High-Fat Meat, 1 Fat
Carbohydrate Choices: 3

Hot Chicken Sub

SUPER *Express*

Philly Turkey Panini

8 slices rye or pumpernickel bread, 1/2 inch thick

2 tablespoons margarine or butter, softened

1/2 pound thinly sliced cooked deli turkey or chicken

4 slices (1 ounce each) mozzarella cheese

1 Spread one side of each bread slice with margarine. Place 4 bread slices margarine sides down in 12-inch skillet; top with turkey and cheese. Top with remaining bread slices, margarine sides up.

2 Cover and cook sandwiches over medium heat 4 to 5 minutes, turning once, until bread is crisp and cheese is melted.

Betty's Tip 4 You

Now you can make this take-out favorite at home in just minutes. Make it Italian by adding basil, pesto and slices of tomatoes.

Nutrition Information

1 SANDWICH: Calories 320 (Calories from Fat 195); Fat 14g (Saturated 5g); Cholesterol 45mg; Sodium 1240mg; Carbohydrate 27g (Dietary Fiber 3g, Sugars 3g); Protein 22g

% Daily Value: Vitamin A 10%; Vitamin C 0%; Calcium 24%; Iron 10%
Diet Exchanges: 2 Starch, 2 Lean Meat, 1 Fat
Carbohydrate Choices: 2

Philly Turkey Panini

Honey-Mustard Chicken Sandwiches

1/4 cup Dijon mustard

2 tablespoons honey

4 boneless, skinless chicken breast halves (about 1 1/4 pounds)

4 whole-grain sandwich buns, split

1 Heat coals or gas grill for direct heat.

2 Mix mustard, honey and 1/8 teaspoon pepper. Brush on chicken. Cover and grill chicken 4 to 6 inches from medium heat 15 to 20 minutes, brushing frequently with mustard mixture and turning occasionally, until juice of chicken is no longer pink when centers of thickest pieces are cut. Discard any remaining mustard mixture.

3 Serve chicken on buns.

Betty's Tip 4 You

Round out the meal with deli fruit salad and frozen French fries—you'll have plenty of time to bake the fries while the chicken breasts cook. If you have honey mustard on hand, use 1/4 cup for the Dijon mustard and the honey.

Nutrition Information

1 SANDWICH: Calories 280 (Calories from Fat 55); Fat 6g (Saturated 1g); Cholesterol 75mg; Sodium 630mg; Carbohydrate 25g (Dietary Fiber 3g, Sugars 8g); Protein 31g

% Daily Value: Vitamin A 0%; Vitamin C 0%; Calcium 4%; Iron 12%
Diet Exchanges: 1 1/2 Starch, 4 Very Lean Meat, 1/2 Fat
Carbohydrate Choices: 1 1/2

Quick Chicken Barbecue Sandwiches

1 cup barbecue sauce

3 packages (2.5 ounces each) sliced smoked chicken, cut into 1-inch strips (3 cups)

6 hamburger buns, split

1 Mix barbecue sauce and chicken in 2-quart saucepan. Heat to boiling; reduce heat to low. Cover and simmer about 5 minutes or until hot.

2 Fill buns with chicken mixture.

Betty's Tip
4 You

If you have leftover cooked or grilled chicken, this is a great way to use it. Cut it into pieces and heat in the barbecue sauce.

Nutrition Information

1 SANDWICH: Calories 215 (Calories from Fat 25); Fat 3g (Saturated 1g); Cholesterol 15mg; Sodium 1080mg; Carbohydrate 37g (Dietary Fiber 1g, Sugars 17g); Protein 10g

% Daily Value: Vitamin A 2%; Vitamin C 0%; Calcium 8%; Iron 10%
Diet Exchanges: 2 1/2 Starch, 1/2 Very Lean Meat
Carbohydrate Choices: 2 1/2

⏱ **SUPER** *Express*

Broiled Bean Sandwiches

4 French rolls

1 cup refried beans

1/2 cup shredded Cheddar cheese (1 ounce)

1 Set oven control to broil. Cut rolls horizontally in half. Broil cut sides up 2 to 3 inches from heat about 1 minute or until golden brown.

2 Spread each roll half with 2 tablespoons beans. Sprinkle each with 1 tablespoon cheese.

3 Broil with tops 2 to 3 inches from heat about 1 1/2 minutes or until cheese is melted.

Betty's Tip 4 You

Slash the fat by using fat-free refried beans and low-fat cheese to enjoy these fiber-rich, open-face sandwiches guilt free.

Nutrition Information
1 SANDWICH: Calories 190 (Calories from Fat 45); Fat 5g (Saturated 2g); Cholesterol 10mg; Sodium 500mg; Carbohydrate 32g (Dietary Fiber 5g, Sugars 1g); Protein 9g

% Daily Value: Vitamin A 2%; Vitamin C 2%; Calcium 8%; Iron 12%
Diet Exchanges: 2 Starch, 1/2 Lean Meat
Carbohydrate Choices: 2

Caramelized-Onion Focaccia Wedges

3 tablespoons margarine or butter

2 medium onions, sliced

8 slices (1 ounce each) provolone or Colby-Monterey Jack cheese

1 round focaccia bread (10 to 12 inches in diameter), cut horizontally in half

1 Heat margarine in a 10-inch skillet over medium-low heat. Cook onions in margarine 15 to 20 minutes, stirring occasionally, until onions are brown and caramelized; remove from heat.

2 Heat oven to 350°. Place half of the cheese on bottom half of focaccia. Top with onions and remaining cheese. Replace top of focaccia. Wrap tightly in aluminum foil. Bake 15 to 20 minutes or until cheese is melted. Cool for 5 minutes. Cut into wedges.

Betty's Tip 4 You

Because caramelizing brings out the natural sweetness of the onions, there's no need to pay extra for specialty sweet onions. Standard yellow onions will do the trick!

Nutrition Information

1 SERVING: Calories 275 (Calories from Fat 135); Fat 15g (Saturated 7g); Cholesterol 30mg; Sodium 650mg; Carbohydrate 26g (Dietary Fiber 1g, Sugars 2g); Protein 9g

% Daily Value: Vitamin A 8%; Vitamin C 0%; Calcium 16%; Iron 8%
Diet Exchanges: 2 Starch, 1/2 High-Fat Meat, 1 1/2 Fat
Carbohydrate Choices: 2

Double-Decker Grilled Cheese Sandwiches

3 tablespoons margarine or butter, softened

8 slices bread

4 slices (1 ounce each) Cheddar cheese

4 slices (1 ounce each) Monterey Jack or mozzarella cheese

1 Spread margarine evenly on one side of each slice of bread.

2 Place 4 slices of bread, buttered sides down, in 12-inch skillet. Top each with 1 slice of Cheddar cheese and 1 slice of Monterey Jack cheese. Top with remaining bread, buttered sides up.

3 Cook uncovered over medium heat about 5 minutes or until the bottoms of the sandwiches are golden brown; turn. Cook 2 to 3 minutes longer or until the bottoms are golden brown and cheese is melted.

Betty's Tip 4 You

This sandwich is very variable. **Try other cheese combinations such as Swiss and mozzarella or dilled Havarti and mozzarella. And if you like, add a slice of tomato before grilling or a couple of strips of cooked sliced bacon.**

Nutrition Information

1 SANDWICH: Calories 425 (Calories from Fat 250); Fat 28g (Saturated 17g); Cholesterol 80mg; Sodium 680mg; Carbohydrate 25g (Dietary Fiber 1g, Sugars 3g); Protein 18g

% Daily Value: Vitamin A 18%; Vitamin C 0%; Calcium 40%; Iron 10%
Diet Exchanges: 1 1/2 Starch, 2 High-Fat Meat, 2 Fat
Carbohydrate Choices: 1 1/2

Double-Decker Grilled Cheese Sandwiches

SUPER *Express*

Italian Vegetable Focaccia Sandwich

1 round focaccia bread (10 to 12 inches in diameter), cut horizontally in half

1 1/2 cups shredded mozzarella or smoked provolone cheese (6 ounces), divided

1 bag (1 pound) frozen broccoli, cauliflower and carrots, thawed and drained (or other combination)

3 tablespoons fat-free Italian dressing

1 Heat oven to 400°.

2 Place bottom half of focaccia on ungreased cookie sheet. Sprinkle with 3/4 cup of the cheese. Spread vegetables over cheese; drizzle with dressing. Sprinkle with remaining 3/4 cup cheese. Replace top of focaccia.

3 Bake 12 to 15 minutes or until golden brown. Cut into wedges.

Betty's Tip 4 You

Focaccia bread, a flavorful Italian flatbread, **is** often available in different flavors, such as herb or olive. Try a new flavor when you shop for the bread—it's generally available in the bakery section of most grocery stores. If it's not there, check the frozen food section.

Nutrition Information

1 SANDWICH: Calories 450 (Calories from Fat 155); Fat 17g (Saturated 6g); Cholesterol 25mg; Sodium 1230mg; Carbohydrate 54g (Dietary Fiber 5g, Sugars 4g); Protein 20g

% Daily Value: Vitamin A 68%; Vitamin C 30%; Calcium 36%; Iron 20%
Diet Exchanges: 3 Starch, 1 High-Fat Meat, 2 Vegetable, 1 1/2 Fat
Carbohydrate Choices: 3 1/2

Mozzarella and Tomato Melts

SUPER *Express*

4 slices Italian bread, each 1 inch thick

8 ounces mozzarella cheese, sliced

2 medium tomatoes, thinly sliced

1/2 cup pesto

1 Set oven control to broil. Place bread on ungreased cookie sheet. Broil with tops about 4 inches from heat until golden brown; turn. Divide cheese among bread slices. Broil just until cheese begins to melt.

2 Arrange tomatoes on cheese; sprinkle with salt and pepper. Top with pesto.

Betty's Tip 4 You

If you have leftover pesto when you make this sandwich, just pop it in the freezer. Pesto can be frozen for up to 6 months. When you're ready to use it again, let it stand covered at room temperature until thawed, at least 4 hours, or throw it in the refrigerator overnight.

Nutrition Information

1 SANDWICH: Calories 390 (Calories from Fat 245); Fat 27g (Saturated 10g); Cholesterol 35mg; Sodium 700mg; Carbohydrate 16g (Dietary Fiber 2g, Sugars 2g); Protein 21g

% Daily Value: Vitamin A 22%; Vitamin C 10%; Calcium 54%; Iron 10%
Diet Exchanges: 1 Starch, 2 1/2 High-Fat Meat, 1 1/2 Fat
Carbohydrate Choices: 1

SUPER *Express*

Peanut Butter and Banana Wraps

1/2 cup creamy peanut butter

4 whole wheat or regular flour tortillas (8 to 10 inches in diameter)

1/4 cup honey

2 small bananas, sliced

1 Spread 2 tablespoons of the peanut butter evenly over each tortilla. Drizzle 1 tablespoon of the honey over each tortilla. Top with banana slices.

2 Roll up tortillas. Secure with toothpicks.

Betty's Tip
4 You

These wraps would be fun for the kids' lunch bags. To keep sliced bananas from turning brown, just dip into lemon or orange juice before assembling the wraps.

Nutrition Information

1 WRAP: Calories 395 (Calories from Fat 160); Fat 18g (Saturated 4g); Cholesterol 0mg; Sodium 330mg; Carbohydrate 52g (Dietary Fiber 6g, Sugars 26g); Protein 12g

% Daily Value: Vitamin A 0%; Vitamin C 8%; Calcium 2%; Iron 10% **Diet Exchanges:** 2 1/2 Starch, 1/2 High-Fat Meat, 1 Fruit, 2 Fat **Carbohydrate Choices:** 3 1/2

Vegetable Tortillas

1 small red or yellow bell pepper, chopped (1/2 cup)

1/2 cup chopped chayote

6 fat-free flour tortillas (6 to 8 inches in diameter)

1 1/2 cups shredded reduced-fat Monterey Jack cheese (6 ounces)

1 Mix bell pepper and chayote. Spoon 1/4 cup of the vegetable mixture onto center of each tortilla.

2 Top each with 1/4 cup of the cheese. Roll tortilla tightly around vegetable mixture.

3 Spray 10-inch nonstick skillet with cooking spray; heat over medium heat. Cook 2 filled tortillas, seam sides down, in skillet about 3 minutes or until bottoms are light brown. Spray tops of tortillas lightly with cooking spray; turn tortillas. Cook about 3 minutes longer or until bottoms are light brown. Repeat with remaining tortillas.

Betty's Tip 4 You

Make this restaurant favorite at home. **Pick up a pack of flavored tortillas, then make exciting new flavors and colors. If you can't find chayote, use zucchini or yellow squash—it will be equally tasty.**

Nutrition Information

1 SANDWICH: Calories 185 (Calories from Fat 65); Fat 7g (Saturated 4g); Cholesterol 20mg; Sodium 410mg; Carbohydrate 16g (Dietary Fiber 1g, Sugars 1g); Protein 15g

% Daily Value: Vitamin A 10%; Vitamin C 12%; Calcium 36%; Iron 4%
Diet Exchanges: 1 Starch, 2 Lean Meat
Carbohydrate Choices: 1

Beef 'n Cheese Calzone

1 can (10 ounces) refrigerated pizza crust dough

1/3 pound thinly sliced cooked roast beef or ham

1 can (4 ounces) mushroom pieces and stems, drained

3/4 cup shredded cheese (mozzarella or Cheddar)

1 Heat oven to 350°. Lightly grease cookie sheet. Unroll pizza crust on cookie sheet; gently stretch to form 12-inch circle.

2 Layer beef, mushrooms and cheese on half of crust to within 1 inch of edge. Fold crust over filling; fold edge up and seal with fork. Cut slits in top.

3 Bake 20 to 25 minutes or until crust is golden brown and filling is hot. Cool 5 minutes before cutting into wedges.

Betty's Tip 4 You

Our version of the popular Italian stuffed pizza is conveniently made using refrigerated pizza crust dough and roast beef from the deli. It's a fast and flavorful way to a good, hot sandwich. Heat some spaghetti or pizza sauce for dipping or serve it with Dijon mustard for extra taste appeal.

Nutrition Information

1 SERVING: Calories 360 (Calories from Fat 15); Fat 14g (Saturated 5g); Cholesterol 40mg; Sodium 590mg; Carbohydrate 37g (Dietary Fiber 2g, Sugars 2g); Protein 21g

% Daily Value: Vitamin A 4%; Vitamin C 0%; Calcium 16%; Iron 20%
Diet Exchanges: 2 1/2 Starch, 2 Medium-Fat Meat
Carbohydrate Choices: 2 1/2

Ranchero Beef Pizza

1 ready-to-serve pizza crust, 12 to 14 inches in diameter

3 cups shredded smoked or regular Cheddar cheese (12 ounces)

1/2 tub (32 ounce size) fully cooked barbecue sauce with sliced beef

4 slices red onion, separated into rings

1 Heat oven to 400°.

2 Place pizza crust on ungreased cookie sheet. Sprinkle with 1 cup of the cheese. Top with beef mixture and onion. Sprinkle with remaining 2 cups cheese.

3 Bake 15 to 20 minutes or until hot.

Betty's Tip 4 You

Look for fully cooked and sliced barbecued beef in the refrigerated meat section or deli of your grocery store.

Nutrition Information

1 SERVING: Calories 650 (Calories from Fat 260); Fat 29g (Saturated 15g); Cholesterol 80mg; Sodium 1270mg; Carbohydrate 69g (Dietary Fiber 2g, Sugars 16g); Protein 28g

% Daily Value: Vitamin A 14%; Vitamin C 2%; Calcium 32%; Iron 24%
Diet Exchanges: 4 1/2 Starch, 2 High-Fat Meat, 2 Fat
Carbohydrate Choices: 4 1/2

SUPER *Express*

BBQ Chicken Pizza

3 packages (8 ounces each) Italian pizza crusts, or 6 pita breads (6 inches in diameter)

3/4 cup barbecue sauce

1 1/2 cups cut-up cooked chicken

3/4 cup shredded smoked or regular Cheddar cheese (3 ounces)

1 Heat oven to 450°.

2 Place bread shells on ungreased large cookie sheet. Spread barbecue sauce on pizza crusts to within 1/4 inch of edges. Top with chicken and cheese.

3 Bake 7 to 12 minutes or until cheese is melted.

Betty's Tip 4 You

Purchased pizza crust, precooked chicken **and** shredded cheese make this one of the easiest pizzas you'll ever make. Add extra zest by sprinkling the pizza with 6 tablespoons of chopped red onion.

Nutrition Information

1 SERVING: Calories 465 (Calories from Fat 100); Fat 11g (Saturated 5g); Cholesterol 45mg; Sodium 1090mg; Carbohydrate 68g (Dietary Fiber 3g, Sugars 9g); Protein 23g

% Daily Value: Vitamin A 4%; Vitamin C 0%; Calcium 18%; Iron 22%
Diet Exchanges: 4 1/2 Starch, 1 1/2 Medium-Fat Meat
Carbohydrate Choices: 4 1/2

BBQ Chicken Pizza

Pizza Monterey

1 can (10 ounces) refrigerated pizza crust dough

2 cups shredded reduced-fat Monterey Jack cheese (8 ounces)

1 bag (1 pound) frozen broccoli, cauliflower and carrots, thawed and drained (or other combination)

1/2 cup reduced-fat ranch dressing

1 Heat oven to 425°. Lightly grease 12-inch pizza pan or rectangular pan, 13 × 9 × 2 inches.

2 Unroll pizza crust dough; press evenly into pan. Bake about 10 minutes or until light golden brown.

3 Sprinkle 1 cup of the cheese over crust. Cut large pieces of vegetables into bite-size pieces if necessary. Spread vegetables over cheese. Drizzle with dressing. Sprinkle with remaining 1 cup cheese.

4 Bake 12 to 15 minutes or until crust is deep golden brown and cheese is melted.

Betty's Tip 4 You

Refrigerated pizza dough and frozen vegetables let you make this pizza very quickly! If the vegetable mixture doesn't excite you, go ahead and use the combination you like—the recipe will work just fine.

Nutrition Information

1 SERVING: Calories 315 (Calories from Fat 125); Fat 14g (Saturated 5g); Cholesterol 20mg; Sodium 740mg; Carbohydrate 30g (Dietary Fiber 3g, Sugars 4g); Protein 17g

% Daily Value: Vitamin A 50%; Vitamin C 20%; Calcium 36%; Iron 10%
Diet Exchanges: 2 Starch, 1 1/2 Medium-Fat Meat, 1 Fat
Carbohydrate Choices: 3

Easy Bagel Pizzas

1 cup pizza sauce

8 bagels, split

2 cups shredded mozzarella cheese
(8 ounces)

Assorted toppings (sliced
mushrooms, sliced ripe olives,
chopped zucchini or chopped
bell pepper)

1 Heat oven to 425°. Spread 1 tablespoon pizza sauce over each
bagel half. Sprinkle each with 1 tablespoon of the cheese.

2 Arrange topping on pizzas. Sprinkle with remaining cheese.
Place on ungreased cookie sheet. Bake 5 to 10 minutes or until
cheese is melted.

Betty's Tip
4 You

These bagel sandwiches are great in the microwave! Toast the bagel halves first, then arrange toppings and cheese on the bagels. Place 4 bagel halves on a
microwavable paper plate. Cover loosely and microwave on
High 30 seconds or until cheese is melted. Repeat with remaining bagels.

Nutrition Information

1 SERVING: Calories 255 (Calories from Fat 65); Fat 7g
(Saturated 3g); Cholesterol 15mg; Sodium 610mg;
Carbohydrate 34g (Dietary Fiber 2g, Sugars 2g); Protein 14g

% Daily Value: Vitamin A 10%; Vitamin C 10%; Calcium 26%; Iron 14%
Diet Exchanges: 2 Starch, 1 Medium-Fat Meat, 1 Vegetable
Carbohydrate Choices: 2

4 Star Ideas

Fast and Flavorful

Do you have stir-fry sauces and vegetables in the refrigerator? Here are some quick ideas using those ingredients for busy cooks like you:

★ Top your turkey patties with Hawaiian stir-fry sauce and cooked stir-fry vegetables

★ Stir-fry chicken strips with frozen chop-suey vegetables, sliced mushrooms and Hoisin sauce

★ Sweeten up your chicken breasts with duck sauce or sweet-and-sour sauce, diced green peppers and pineapple chunks

★ Spice up your summer squash and zucchini with chile powder, picante sauce and lime juice

4 Star Ideas

Saucy Ideas

Start with a pantry staple and add pizzazz! With these tasty suggestions, you can turn simple meats into sensational dinners:

★ Sprinkle curry powder on your meat. Serve with yogurt mixed with chopped green onions and cucumbers.

★ Add Cajun/Creole seasoning to bread crumbs and sprinkle on chicken. Serve with canned black beans and corn.

★ Make a marinade of lime juice and Caribbean jerk sauce for fish. Serve fish with fresh mango slices.

★ Sprinkle lemon pepper on your chicken breasts, steaks or fish fillets for seasoning. Sauté in olive oil with white wine or broth.

4

Memorable Main Skillet Meals and Stir-Fries

(🕐) Breaded Pork Chops   92

Pork with Caramelized Onions   94

Skillet Apple-Butter Pork Chops   95

(🕐) Bratwurst and Sauerkraut   96

Italian Sausage Skillet   97

Sloppy Joes with Potatoes and Onion   98

Mediterranean Skillet Chicken   99

Easy Mexican Chicken and Beans   100

(🕐) Lemon-Pistachio Chicken   102

(🕐) Mozzarella-Topped Chicken and Eggplant   104

(🕐) Ranch Chicken   105

One-Pan Potatoes and Chicken   106

Skillet-Fried Chicken   108

(🕐) Teriyaki Chicken Stir-Fry   110

(🕐) Vegetable-Chicken Stir-Fry   111

Honey Mustard Turkey with Snap Peas   112

Glazed Turkey Tenderloins   114

Maple-Glazed Turkey Breast   115

(🕐) Garlic Shrimp   116

(🕐) Lemon-Dill Shrimp   117

Panfried Fish Fillets   118

Ramen Stir-Fry   119

Photos: opposite top: Ranch Chicken (page 105); opposite bottom: Honey Mustard Turkey with Snap Peas (page 112) | (🕐) **Super**Express *ready in 20 minutes or less*

SUPER *Express*

Breaded Pork Chops

1/2 cup Original Bisquick® mix

12 saltine crackers, crushed (1/2 cup)

1 egg

8 pork boneless loin chops, 1/2 inch thick (about 2 pounds)

1 Mix Bisquick, cracker crumbs, 1 teaspoon salt and 1/4 teaspoon pepper. Mix egg and 2 tablespoons of water.

2 Dip pork into egg mixture, then coat with Bisquick mixture.

3 Spray 12-inch skillet with cooking spray; heat over medium-high heat. Cook pork in skillet 8 to 10 minutes, turning once, until slightly pink in center.

Betty's Tip 4 You

Try using seasoned salt on the pork chops for extra flavor, and then complete dinner by serving boiled potatoes and steamed green beans.

Nutrition Information
1 SERVING: Calories 220 (Calories from Fat 90); Fat 10g (Saturated 3g); Cholesterol 90mg; Sodium 500mg; Carbohydrate 8g (Dietary Fiber 0g, Sugars 1g); Protein 24g

% Daily Value: Vitamin A 0%; Vitamin C 0%; Calcium 2%; Iron 6%
Diet Exchanges: 1/2 Starch, 2 1/2 Lean Meat
Carbohydrate Choices: 1/2

Breaded Pork Chops

Pork with Caramelized Onions

1 pound pork tenderloin

1/4 teaspoon paprika

1 large onion, thinly sliced

1/4 teaspoon sugar

1 Remove fat from pork. Cut pork into 1/2-inch slices. Sprinkle 1/2 teaspoon of salt and paprika over both sides of pork.

2 Spray 10-inch nonstick skillet with cooking spray; heat over medium-high heat. Cook pork in skillet 6 to 8 minutes, turning once, until no longer pink. Remove pork from skillet; cover and keep warm. Remove skillet from heat.

3 Spray skillet with cooking spray; heat over medium-high heat. Cook onion in skillet 1 minute, stirring frequently. Reduce heat to medium. Stir in sugar. Cook about 3 minutes longer, stirring frequently, until onion is soft and golden brown. Spoon over pork.

Betty's Tip 4 You

The tenderloin is considered the choicest of pork cuts. Although higher in price per pound than loin roast, tenderloin is a good value because it is lean and has no taste.

Nutrition Information

1 SERVING: Calories 155 (Calories from Fat 35); Fat 4g (Saturated 2g); Cholesterol 70mg; Sodium 350mg; Carbohydrate 4g (Dietary Fiber 1g, Sugars 2g); Protein 26g

% Daily Value: Vitamin A 0%; Vitamin C 2%; Calcium 0%; Iron 8%
Diet Exchanges: 4 Very Lean Meat, 1/2 Fat
Carbohydrate Choices: 0

Skillet Apple-Butter Pork Chops

**4 pork loin or rib chops,
each 1/2 inch thick**

6 tablespoons apple butter

**6 tablespoons onion,
finely chopped**

1 Spray nonstick 12-inch skillet with cooking spray; heat over medium heat. Sprinkle both sides of pork with salt and pepper. Cook pork in skillet about 5 minutes, turning once, until brown.

2 Mix apple butter and onion; spoon over pork in skillet. Heat to boiling; reduce heat. Cover and simmer 10 to 15 minutes, stirring and turning pork occasionally, until pork is slightly pink in center near bone.

Betty's Tip
4 You

Like the apple butter? Try these quick pork chops with other flavored butters, such as pumpkin butter. Or try them with sliced peaches or pears.

Nutrition Information

1 SERVING: Calories 225 (Calories from Fat 70); Fat 8g (Saturated 3g); Cholesterol 65mg; Sodium 340mg; Carbohydrate 15g (Dietary Fiber 1g, Sugars 12g); Protein 23g

% Daily Value: Vitamin A 0%; Vitamin C 2%; Calcium 0%; Iron 4%
Diet Exchanges: 3 Lean Meat, 1 Fruit
Carbohydrate Choices: 1

Super *Express*

Bratwurst and Sauerkraut

1 tablespoon margarine or butter

1 pound fully cooked bratwurst

2 cans (16 ounces each) sauerkraut, drained

1/3 cup packed brown sugar

1 Melt margarine in 10-inch skillet over medium heat. Cook bratwurst in margarine, turning frequently, until brown, about 5 minutes.

2 Add sauerkraut; sprinkle with brown sugar. Cover and cook over low heat until hot, about 10 minutes.

Betty's Tip 4 You

This German-inspired dish also works well in the microwave. To microwave, omit the margarine. Arrange bratwurst in an ungreased square microwavable dish, 8 × 8 × 2 inches. Add sauerkraut; sprinkle with brown sugar. Cover with vented plastic wrap and microwave on High, rotating dish 1/2 turn every 5 minutes, until hot, 10 to 12 minutes.

Nutrition Information
1 SERVING: Calories 325 (Calories from Fat 205); Fat 23g (Saturated 8g); Cholesterol 45mg; Sodium 1790mg; Carbohydrate 20g (Dietary Fiber 4g, Sugars 13g); Protein 10g

% Daily Value: Vitamin A 2%; Vitamin C 18%; Calcium 6%; Iron 16%
Diet Exchanges: 1 1/2 High-Fat Meat, 1 Vegetable, 1 Fruit, 1 1/2 Fat
Carbohydrate Choices: 1

Italian Sausage Skillet

1 pound bulk Italian sausage

3/4 cup sliced fresh mushrooms
(2 ounces)

1/2 large red onion, cut into
1/8-inch slices

1 small green bell pepper, chopped
(1/2 cup)

1 Cook sausage in 10-inch skillet over medium-high heat about 10 minutes, stirring occasionally, until no longer pink in center; drain.

2 Stir in mushrooms and onion; reduce heat. Cover and simmer about 10 minutes, stirring occasionally, until vegetables are tender. Stir in bell pepper. Cover and simmer about 5 minutes or until bell pepper is crisp-tender.

Betty's Tip 4 You

This sausage and vegetable combo can be served so many ways—toss with your favorite pasta, serve it over white or brown rice, put it into a submarine bun or enjoy it by itself.

Nutrition Information

1 SERVING: Calories 275 (Calories from Fat 190); Fat 21g (Saturated 8g); Cholesterol 65mg; Sodium 760mg; Carbohydrate 5g (Dietary Fiber 1g, Sugars 2g); Protein 17g

% Daily Value: Vitamin A 2%; Vitamin C 16%; Calcium 2%; Iron 8%
Diet Exchanges: 2 1/2 High-Fat Meat, 1 Vegetable
Carbohydrate Choices: 0

Sloppy Joes with Potatoes and Onion

1 pound lean ground beef

1 medium onion, sliced and separated into rings

2 medium potatoes, thinly sliced

1 can (15 1/2 ounces) Sloppy Joe sauce

1 Crumble ground beef into 10-inch skillet; sprinkle with salt and pepper. Layer onion and potatoes on beef; pour sauce over top.

2 Cover and cook over low heat until beef is done and potatoes are tender, about 30 minutes.

Betty's Tip 4 You

Try this homey dish in the microwave. Crumble ground beef into 2-quart microwavable casserole; sprinkle with salt and pepper. Layer onion and potatoes on beef. Cover tightly and microwave on High 5 minutes; rotate casserole 1/2 turn. Microwave 5 minutes longer. Pour sauce over potatoes. Cover tightly and microwave 5 minutes; rotate casserole 1/2 turn. Microwave until potatoes are tender, 5 or 6 minutes longer.

Nutrition Information

1 SERVING: Calories 425 (Calories from Fat 155); Fat 17g (Saturated 6g); Cholesterol 65mg; Sodium 1320mg; Carbohydrate 44g (Dietary Fiber 3g, Sugars 28g); Protein 24g

% Daily Value: Vitamin A 28%; Vitamin C 18%; Calcium 4%; Iron 16%
Diet Exchanges: 3 Starch, 2 Medium-Fat Meat, 1 Fat
Carbohydrate Choices: 3

Mediterranean Skillet Chicken

2 tablespoons olive or vegetable oil

4 boneless, skinless chicken breast halves (1 pound)

1 can (14 1/2 ounces) Italian-style stewed tomatoes, undrained

1/2 cup sliced ripe olives

1 Heat oil in 12-inch nonstick skillet over medium-high heat. Cook chicken in oil 5 minutes, turning once, until brown.

2 Stir in remaining ingredients. Heat to boiling; reduce heat to low. Cover and simmer 15 to 20 minutes or until juice of chicken is no longer pink when centers of thickest pieces are cut.

Betty's Tip 4 You

It only takes four ingredients to catch the flavors of the Mediterranean! The chicken is delicious served with orzo or couscous. For added flavor, stir in a teaspoon of grated lemon peel to the orzo or couscous or into the chicken dish.

Nutrition Information

1 SERVING: Calories 260 (Calories from Fat 115); Fat 13g (Saturated 2g); Cholesterol 75mg; Sodium 500mg; Carbohydrate 8g (Dietary Fiber 1g, Sugars 5g); Protein 28g

% Daily Value: Vitamin A 6%; Vitamin C 10%; Calcium 4%; Iron 10%
Diet Exchanges: 4 Lean Meat, 1 Vegetable
Carbohydrate Choices: 1/2

Easy Mexican Chicken and Beans

1 pound cut-up boneless chicken breast for stir-fry

1 envelope (1 1/4 ounces) taco seasoning mix

1 can (15 to 16 ounces) black or pinto beans, rinsed and drained

1 can (11 ounces) whole kernel corn with red and green peppers, undrained

1 Spray 10-inch nonstick skillet with cooking spray. Cook chicken in skillet over medium-high heat 8 to 10 minutes, stirring occasionally, until no longer pink in center.

2 Stir in seasoning mix, beans, corn and 1/4 cup of water. Cook uncovered over medium-high heat 8 to 10 minutes, stirring frequently, until sauce is slightly thickened.

Betty's Tip 4 You

Turn this dish into a weeknight fiesta! **Serve with flour tortillas, sour cream, salsa, black olives and green chilies and let everyone make their own wrap.**

Nutrition Information

1 SERVING: Calories 350 (Calories from Fat 45); Fat 5g (Saturated 1g); Cholesterol 70mg; Sodium 1020mg; Carbohydrate 48g (Dietary Fiber 9g, Sugars 9g); Protein 37g

% Daily Value: Vitamin A 18%; Vitamin C 10%; Calcium 12%; Iron 22%
Diet Exchanges: 3 Starch, 4 Very Lean Meat
Carbohydrate Choices: 3

Easy Mexican Chicken and Beans

SUPER *Express*

Lemon-Pistachio Chicken

4 boneless, skinless chicken breast halves (about 1 1/4 pounds)

1 tablespoon olive or vegetable oil

3 tablespoons lemon juice

1/4 cup chopped pistachio nuts, toasted

1 Flatten each chicken breast half to 1/4-inch thickness between sheets of plastic wrap or waxed paper. Sprinkle both side of chicken with 1 teaspoon of pepper.

2 Heat oil in 12-inch skillet over medium-high heat. Cook chicken and lemon juice in oil 10 to 15 minutes, turning chicken once and stirring juice mixture occasionally, until juice of chicken is no longer pink when centers of thickest pieces are cut. Serve chicken topped with any remaining pan juices and nuts.

Betty's Tip 4 You

Toasting nuts really brings out their flavor. To toast nuts, bake uncovered in ungreased shallow pan in a 350° oven about 10 minutes, stirring occasionally, until golden brown. Or cook in ungreased heavy skillet over medium-low heat 5 to 7 minutes, stirring frequently until browning begins, then stirring constantly until golden brown.

Nutrition Information

1 SERVING: Calories 215 (Calories from Fat 90); Fat 10g (Saturated 2g); Cholesterol 75mg; Sodium 100mg; Carbohydrate 3g (Dietary Fiber 1g, Sugars 1g); Protein 28g

% Daily Value: Vitamin A 0%; Vitamin C 2%; Calcium 2%; Iron 6%
Diet Exchanges: 4 Lean Meat
Carbohydrate Choices: 0

Lemon-Pistachio Chicken

Mozzarella-Topped Chicken and Eggplant

8 boneless, skinless chicken thighs (about 1 1/3 pounds)

1 small eggplant, peeled and cut into 1-inch cubes (4 cups)

1 can (15 ounces) Italian-style tomato sauce

1/2 cup shredded reduced-fat mozzarella cheese (2 ounces)

1 Remove fat from chicken. Spray 12-inch nonstick skillet with cooking spray.

2 Cook chicken and eggplant in skillet over medium heat about 10 minutes, stirring frequently, until juice of chicken is no longer pink when centers of thickest pieces are cut.

3 Stir in tomato sauce and 1/2 teaspoon cracked black pepper; heat through. Remove from heat. Sprinkle with cheese.

Betty's Tip 4 You

This slimmed-down version of chicken and eggplant parmigiana truly saves calories and time. It cuts calories by starting with unbreaded chicken, omitting olive oil for sautéing and using reduced-fat mozzarella. The recipe also saves time by simmering everything quickly in a skillet and taking advantage of Italian-style tomato sauce.

Nutrition Information

1 SERVING: Calories 325 (Calories from Fat 125); Fat 14g (Saturated 5g); Cholesterol 70mg; Sodium 800mg; Carbohydrate 15g (Dietary Fiber 4g, Sugars 8g); Protein 35g

% Daily Value: Vitamin A 20%; Vitamin C 12%; Calcium 16%; Iron 20%
Diet Exchanges: 4 Lean Meat, 3 Vegetable, 1/2 Fat
Carbohydrate Choices: 1

Ranch Chicken

SUPER
Express

4 boneless, skinless chicken breast halves (about 1/4 pound each)

1/4 cup ranch dressing

1/3 cup seasoned dry bread crumbs

2 tablespoons olive or vegetable oil

1 Remove fat from chicken.

2 Pour the dressing into a shallow bowl or pie pan. Place the bread crumbs on waxed paper or a plate.

3 Dip chicken, one piece at a time, into dressing, coating all sides. Then coat all sides with bread crumbs.

4 Heat oil in 10- or 12-inch skillet over medium-high heat. Cook chicken in oil 12 to 15 minutes, turning once until golden brown and juice is no longer pink when the centers of the thickest pieces are cut.

Betty's Tip 4 You

Keep it simple—pick up a marinated vegetable salad from the grocery deli and brownies from the grocery bakery to complete your meal. For an added treat, top each brownie with a scoop of ice cream and a dollop of chocolate sauce.

Nutrition Information

1 SERVING: Calories 290 (Calories from Fat 145); Fat 16g (Saturated 3g); Cholesterol 80mg; Sodium 290mg; Carbohydrate 8g (Dietary Fiber 0g, Sugars 2g); Protein 28g

% Daily Value: Vitamin A 0%; Vitamin C 0%; Calcium 4%; Iron 8%
Diet Exchanges: 1/2 Starch, 4 Lean Meat, 1/2 Fat
Carbohydrate Choices: 1/2

One-Pan Potatoes and Chicken

2 tablespoons vegetable oil

8 medium red potatoes, thinly sliced

1 pound boneless, skinless chicken breast halves, cut into thin strips

1 medium red bell pepper, cut into thin strips

1 Heat oil in 12-inch nonstick skillet over medium heat. Add potatoes, chicken and bell pepper to skillet. Sprinkle with 1 teaspoon of salt.

2 Cook 15 to 20 minutes, stirring frequently, until chicken is no longer pink in center and potatoes are tender.

Betty's Tip 4 You

A family-pleasing meal, in only 30 minutes! Add coleslaw from the deli and warm apple crisp or make-your-own sundaes for dessert and you have a home-run dinner.

Nutrition Information

1 SERVING: Calories 375 (Calories from Fat 80); Fat 9g (Saturated 2g); Cholesterol 70mg; Sodium 670mg; Carbohydrate 45g (Dietary Fiber 5g, Sugars 3g); Protein 29g

% Daily Value: Vitamin A 2%; Vitamin C 40%; Calcium 2%; Iron 18%
Diet Exchanges: 3 Starch, 3 Very Lean Meat, 1 Fat
Carbohydrate Choices: 3

One-Pan Potatoes and Chicken

Skillet-Fried Chicken

1/2 cup all-purpose flour

1 tablespoon paprika

3- to 3 1/2-pound cut-up
broiler-fryer chicken

Vegetable oil

1   Mix flour, paprika, 1 1/2 teaspoons of salt and 1/2 teaspoon of pepper. Coat chicken with flour mixture.

2   Heat oil (1/4 inch) in 12-inch nonstick skillet over medium-high heat. Cook chicken in oil about 10 minutes or until light brown on all sides; reduce heat to low. Turn chicken skin sides up.

3   Simmer uncovered about 20 minutes, without turning, until juice of chicken is no longer pink when centers of thickest pieces are cut.

Betty's Tip 4 You

Fried chicken is perfect with potato salad and fresh homemade biscuits hot from the oven. This is easy to do with a quick stop at the deli counter and Original Bisquick® mix. For dessert you can't go wrong with apple pie, with or without ice cream.

Nutrition Information

1 SERVING: Calories 315 (Calories from Fat 180); Fat 20g (Saturated 5g); Cholesterol 85mg; Sodium 80mg; Carbohydrate 6g (Dietary Fiber 0g, Sugars 0g); Protein 27g

% Daily Value: Vitamin A 12%; Vitamin C 0%; Calcium 2%; Iron 10%
Diet Exchanges: 4 Medium-Fat Meat
Carbohydrate Choices: 1/2

Skillet-Fried Chicken

SUPER
Express
Teriyaki Chicken Stir-Fry

1 pound cut-up chicken breast for stir-fry

1/2 cup teriyaki baste and glaze

3 tablespoons lemon juice

1 bag (1 pound) frozen broccoli, carrots, water chestnuts and red peppers (or other combination)

1 Spray 12-inch nonstick skillet with cooking spray; heat over medium-high heat. Add chicken; stir-fry 3 to 4 minutes until no longer pink in center.

2 Stir in remaining ingredients. Heat to boiling, stirring constantly; reduce heat. Cover and simmer about 6 minutes or until vegetables are crisp-tender.

Betty's Tip 4 You

This super quick stir-fry is just right **with hot cooked rice or couscous, even hot cooked pasta—** whatever you like best.

Nutrition Information

1 SERVING: Calories 210 (Calories from Fat 35); Fat 4g (Saturated 1g); Cholesterol 70mg; Sodium 1720mg; Carbohydrate 14g (Dietary Fiber 3g, Sugars 6g); Protein 30g

% Daily Value: Vitamin A 22%; Vitamin C 36%; Calcium 6%; Iron 14%
Diet Exchanges: 1/2 Starch, 4 Very Lean Meat, 1 Vegetable
Carbohydrate Choices: 1

Vegetable-Chicken Stir-Fry

1 pound boneless, skinless chicken breast halves or thighs

4 cups cut-up assorted vegetables (bell peppers, broccoli flowerets, shredded carrots)

1 clove garlic, finely chopped

1/2 cup stir-fry sauce

1 Remove fat from chicken. Cut chicken into 1-inch pieces. Spray 12-inch nonstick skillet with cooking spray; heat over medium-high heat. Add chicken; stir-fry about 3 minutes until no longer pink in center. Remove chicken from skillet. Remove skillet from heat.

2 Spray skillet with cooking spray. Add vegetables and garlic; stir-fry about 2 minutes or until vegetables are crisp-tender. Add chicken and stir-fry sauce. Cook and stir about 2 minutes or until hot.

Betty's Tip 4 You

Add toasty crunch with toasted wonton skins!
Cut wonton skins into thin strips, and bake on an ungreased cookie sheet at 350° for 5 to 7 minutes or until light golden brown. Top each serving of this stir-fry with whole or broken toasted wonton strips.

Nutrition Information

1 SERVING: Calories 210 (Calories from Fat 35); Fat 4g (Saturated 1g); Cholesterol 70mg; Sodium 1460mg; Carbohydrate 14g (Dietary Fiber 3g, Sugars 8g); Protein 29g

% Daily Value: Vitamin A 100%; Vitamin C 66%; Calcium 4%; Iron 12%
Diet Exchanges: 4 Very Lean Meat, 2 Vegetable, 1/2 Fat
Carbohydrate Choices: 1

Honey Mustard Turkey with Snap Peas

1 pound uncooked turkey breast slices, about 1/4 inch thick

1/2 cup Dijon and honey poultry and meat marinade

1 cup baby-cut carrots, cut lengthwise in half

2 cups snap pea pods

1 Place the turkey in shallow glass or plastic dish. Pour marinade over turkey; turn slices to coat evenly. Cover and refrigerate 20 minutes.

2 Spray 10-inch skillet with cooking spray; heat over medium heat. Drain most of marinade from turkey. Cook turkey in skillet about 5 minutes, turning once, until brown.

3 Add carrots, lifting turkey to place carrots on bottom of skillet. Top turkey and carrots with pea pods. Cover and cook about 7 minutes or until carrots are tender and turkey is no longer pink in center.

Betty's Tip 4 You

This surefire winner for the weeknight **is a complete meal in a skillet, and it's an easy way to give vegetables to your family.** If you like, serve with a crusty bread, or rice.

Nutrition Information

1 SERVING: Calories 195 (Calories from Fat 65); Fat 7g (Saturated 2g); Cholesterol 65mg; Sodium 190mg; Carbohydrate 8g (Dietary Fiber 2g, Sugars 5g); Protein 25g

% Daily Value: Vitamin A 100%; Vitamin C 14%; Calcium 4%; Iron 10%
Diet Exchanges: 3 Very Lean Meat, 2 Vegetable, 1 Fat
Carbohydrate Choices: 1/2

Honey Mustard Turkey with Snap Peas

Glazed Turkey Tenderloins

1 pound turkey breast tenderloin

1/3 cup orange marmalade spreadable fruit

1 teaspoon finely chopped gingerroot or 1/2 teaspoon ground ginger

1 teaspoon Worcestershire sauce

1 Spray 10-inch nonstick skillet with cooking spray. Cook turkey in skillet over medium heat about 5 minutes or until brown; turn. Stir in remaining ingredients; reduce heat.

2 Cover and simmer about 15 minutes, stirring sauce occasionally, until sauce is thickened and juice of turkey is no longer pink when thickest part is cut.

3 Cut turkey into thin slices. Spoon sauce over turkey.

Betty's Tip 4 You

Any remaining turkey makes for a super sandwich. **Top with sliced provolone or Monterey Jack cheese,** romaine leaves and sliced tomato on your favorite hearty grain bread. Or for more bite, add red pepper rings and thin slices of cucumbers.

Nutrition Information

1 SERVING: Calories 165 (Calories from Fat 10); Fat 1g (Saturated 0g); Cholesterol 75mg; Sodium 60mg; Carbohydrate 13g (Dietary Fiber 0g, Sugars 12g); Protein 26g

% Daily Value: Vitamin A 0%; Vitamin C 0%; Calcium 2%; Iron 8%
Diet Exchanges: 3 1/2 Very Lean Meat, 1 Fruit
Carbohydrate Choices: 1

Maple-Glazed Turkey Breast

1 package (6 ounces) original-flavor long-grain and wild rice mix

1 pound boneless turkey breast

1/4 cup maple-flavored syrup

1/2 cup chopped walnuts

1 Mix uncooked rice, seasoning packet from rice mix and 1 1/4 cups of water in 3 1/2- to 6-quart slow cooker.

2 Place turkey breast, skin side up, on rice mixture. Drizzle with maple syrup. Sprinkle with walnuts.

3 Cover and cook on low heat setting 4 to 5 hours or until juice of turkey is no longer pink when center is cut.

Betty's Tip 4 You

Serve this sweet turkey with cooked dilled carrots and chilled cranberry relish. Pass a basket of warm wheat rolls and honey butter for a chill-chasing autumn meal.

Nutrition Information

1 SERVING: Calories 450 (Calories from Fat 110); Fat 12g (Saturated 2g); Cholesterol 75mg; Sodium 610mg; Carbohydrate 52g (Dietary Fiber 2g, Sugars 8g); Protein 34g

% Daily Value: Vitamin A 2%; Vitamin C 0%; Calcium 4%; Iron 18%
Diet Exchanges: 3 1/2 Starch, 3 Lean Meat
Carbohydrate Choices: 3 1/2

SUPER
Express

Garlic Shrimp

1 tablespoon vegetable oil

3 large cloves garlic, finely chopped

1 pound uncooked peeled deveined medium shrimp, thawed if frozen

1 large carrot, cut into julienne strips (1 cup)

1 Heat nonstick wok or 12-inch nonstick skillet over medium-high heat. Add oil; rotate wok to coat sides.

2 Add garlic; stir-fry 1 minute. Add shrimp; stir-fry 1 minute. Add carrots; stir-fry about 3 minutes or until shrimp are pink and firm and carrot is crisp-tender.

Betty's Tip
4 You

This recipe kicks! The flavor is just as daring as you are, heady from a generous use of garlic. Add a touch of red pepper and chopped parsley for these zesty shrimp. Round out your dinner with hot garlic bread or warm corn bread and pass the jar of honey.

Nutrition Information

1 SERVING: Calories 110 (Calories from Fat 25); Fat 3g (Saturated 1g); Cholesterol 160mg; Sodium 190mg; Carbohydrate 3g (Dietary Fiber 1g, Sugars 1g); Protein 18g

% Daily Value: Vitamin A 70%; Vitamin C 2%; Calcium 4%; Iron 14%
Diet Exchanges: 2 1/2 Very Lean Meat, 1/2 Vegetable
Carbohydrate Choices: 0

Lemon-Dill Shrimp

2 tablespoons lemon juice

1 tablespoon olive or vegetable oil

1 1/2 teaspoons chopped fresh
dill weed

1 pound uncooked peeled deveined
medium shrimp, thawed if frozen

1 Mix lemon juice, oil, dill weed and 1/4 teaspoon salt; set aside.

2 Spray 10-inch nonstick skillet with cooking spray; heat over medium heat. Cook shrimp in skillet over medium heat about 5 minutes, stirring frequently, until pink and firm. Remove shrimp from skillet, using slotted spoon. Drain well on paper towels.

3 Wipe out skillet with paper towel. Add shrimp and lemon juice mixture to skillet. Cook about 1 minute over medium heat, stirring frequently, until heated through.

Betty's Tip
4 You

Give this super-quick and delicious dish a special touch. Dress up the plates with Green Onion Brushes. To make, cut each green onion 2 inches above root; slice off end of root. From root end, make 2 or 3 cuts into onion. Make 2 or 3 more cuts at a right angle to first cuts. Place in ice water until flower opens up.

Nutrition Information
1 SERVING: Calories 100 (Calories from Fat 25); Fat 3g (Saturated 1g); Cholesterol 160mg; Sodium 330mg; Carbohydrate 1g (Dietary Fiber 0g, Sugars 0g); Protein 17g

% Daily Value: Vitamin A 4%; Vitamin C 2%; Calcium 2%; Iron 14%
Diet Exchanges: 2 1/2 Very Lean Meat, 1/2 Fat
Carbohydrate Choices: 0

Panfried Fish Fillets

1 1/2 pounds mild-flavor fish fillets, about 3/4 inch thick

1 egg

1/2 cup all-purpose flour, cornmeal or grated Parmesan cheese

Vegetable oil or shortening

1 Cut fish fillets into 6 serving pieces. Sprinkle both sides of fish with 1/2 teaspoon salt and 1/8 teaspoon pepper.

2 Beat egg and 1 tablespoon of water in shallow bowl until well mixed. Sprinkle flour on waxed paper or a plate. Dip both sides of fish pieces into egg, then coat completely with flour.

3 Heat oil (1/8 inch) in 10-inch skillet over medium heat about 2 minutes. Fry fish in oil 6 to 10 minutes, turning once, until fish flakes easily with fork and is brown on both sides. Drain on paper towels.

Betty's Tip 4 You

Nothing fishy about what to use here! Use any mild-flavored fish that's available, such as flounder, cod, catfish, snapper or halibut.

Nutrition Information
1 SERVING: Calories 155 (Calories from Fat 55); Fat 6g (Saturated 1g); Cholesterol 80mg; Sodium 90mg; Carbohydrate 5g (Dietary Fiber 0g, Sugars 0g); Protein 20g

% Daily Value: Vitamin A 0%; Vitamin C 0%; Calcium 2%; Iron 4%
Diet Exchanges: 3 Lean Meat
Carbohydrate Choices: 0

Ramen Stir-Fry

1 pound beef boneless sirloin

1/4 cup stir-fry sauce

1 package (3 ounces) Oriental-flavor ramen soup mix

1 bag (1 pound) fresh stir-fry vegetables

1 Remove fat from beef. Cut beef into thin strips. Spray 12-inch nonstick skillet with cooking spray; heat over medium-high heat. Cook beef in skillet 3 to 5 minutes, stirring occasionally, until brown. Add stir-fry sauce. Remove beef from skillet.

2 Heat 2 cups of water in skillet. Break up noodles from soup mix into water; stir until slightly softened. Stir in vegetables and Oriental flavor packet.

3 Heat to boiling. Boil 5 to 7 minutes, stirring frequently, until hot.

Betty's Tip 4 You

The stir-fry works well with leftover beef sirloin. Remember this recipe next time you have leftovers from the grill.

Nutrition Information

1 SERVING: Calories 250 (Calories from Fat 65); Fat 7g (Saturated 2g); Cholesterol 60mg; Sodium 1020mg; Carbohydrate 19g (Dietary Fiber 3g, Sugars 5g); Protein 28g

% Daily Value: Vitamin A 12%; Vitamin C 44%; Calcium 4%; Iron 22%
Diet Exchanges: 1 Starch, 3 Very Lean Meat, 1 Vegetable, 1 Fat
Carbohydrate Choices: 1

4 Star Ideas

Make-In-Minutes Marinades

Take a vacation from the ordinary marinated beef roast; these exciting flavor blends make for an extraordinary roast:

★ Combine honey-mustard dressing with ground ginger and soy sauce

★ Mash kiwifruit with crumbled mint, sugar and lime juice

★ Mix dill dip and milk

★ Mix brandy with beef broth, sour cream and chopped shallots

4 Star Ideas

Top-Notch Casseroles

Add extra interest to your casseroles by topping with one of the following:

★ Grated Parmesan cheese

★ Bacon flavor bits

★ Seasoned bread crumbs

★ Chopped garlic, from a jar

Oven All-Star: Roasts and Casseroles

Slow-Cooker Garlic Pork Roast   122

Pork Chops and Apples   124

Italian Roasted Pork Tenderloin   126

Pork Tenderloin with Rosemary   127

Yummy Pork Chops   128

Slow-Cooker Scalloped Potato and Sausage Supper   129

Fiesta Taco Casserole   130

🕐 Lamb with Creamy Mint Sauce   131

Mustard Lamb Chops   132

Honey-Glazed Chicken Breasts   133

Chicken with Cider Glaze   134

Crunchy Oven-Fried Chicken   136

Two-Mustard Chicken   138

Rosemary-Mustard Chicken   140

Slow-Cooker Turkey Sausage Cassoulet   141

Oriental Turkey Patties   142

Oven-Poached Halibut   144

Chili Rice con Queso   145

Lentil and Brown Rice Casserole   146

🕐 Microwave Ravioli Casserole   147

Photos: opposite top: Pork Tenderloin with Rosemary (page 127); opposite bottom: Pork Chops and Apples (page 124)

🕐 **Super**Express *ready in 20 minutes or less*

Slow-Cooker Garlic Pork Roast

3 1/2-pound pork boneless loin roast

1 tablespoon vegetable oil

1 medium onion, sliced

3 cloves garlic, peeled

1 Trim excess fat from pork. Heat oil in 10-inch skillet over medium-high heat. Cook pork in oil about 10 minutes, turning occasionally, until brown on all sides. Sprinkle with 1 teaspoon of salt and 1/2 teaspoon of pepper.

2 Place onion and garlic in 3 1/2- to 6-quart slow cooker. Place pork on onion and garlic. Pour 1 cup of water over pork.

3 Cover and cook on low heat setting 8 to 10 hours or until pork is tender.

*Betty's Tip
4 You*

Jazz up your pork roast with more flavor **by** using chicken broth instead of water and serving with sautéed bell peppers.

Nutrition Information

1 SERVING: Calories 270 (Calories from Fat 125); Fat 14g (Saturated 5g); Cholesterol 100mg; Sodium 300mg; Carbohydrate 1g (Dietary Fiber 0g, Sugars 1g); Protein 35g

% Daily Value: Vitamin A 0%; Vitamin C 0%; Calcium 0%; Iron 6%
Diet Exchanges: 5 Lean Meat
Carbohydrate Choices: 0

Slow-Cooker Garlic Pork Roast

Pork Chops and Apples

1 medium cooking apple,
such as Granny Smith, Wealthy
or Rome Beauty

2 tablespoons packed brown sugar

1/4 teaspoon ground cinnamon

2 pork rib chops, 1/2- to 3/4-inch
thick (about 1/4 pound each)

1 Heat the oven to 350°.

2 Cut the apple into fourths and remove the seeds. Cut each fourth
into 3 to 4 wedges. Place apple wedges in a 1 1/2-quart casserole.
Sprinkle the brown sugar and cinnamon over the apples.

3 Cut most of the fat from pork chops. Spray an 8-inch skillet
with cooking spray, and heat over medium heat 1 to 2 minutes.
Cook pork chops in hot skillet about 5 minutes, turning once,
until light brown.

4 Place the pork chops in a single layer on the apple wedges in
casserole. Cover with lid or aluminum foil and bake about
45 minutes or until pork is slightly pink when cut near bone
and apples are tender.

Betty's Tip
4 You

Round out your pork chops with mixed field
greens with a honey Dijon dressing and warm
rolls. For dessert, top scoops of lemon sorbet with fresh sliced
strawberries.

Nutrition Information

1 SERVING: Calories 235 (Calories from Fat 65); Fat 7g
(Saturated 2g); Cholesterol 55mg; Sodium 40mg; Carbohydrate
24g (Dietary Fiber 2g, Sugars 23g); Protein 19g

% Daily Value: Vitamin A 0%; Vitamin C 2%; Calcium 2%; Iron 6%
Diet Exchanges: 3 Very Lean Meat, 1 1/2 Fruit, 1 Fat
Carbohydrate Choices: 1 1/2

Pork Chops and Apples

Italian Roasted Pork Tenderloin

**2 pork tenderloins,
about 3/4 pound each**

1 teaspoon olive or vegetable oil

1/2 teaspoon fennel seed, crushed

1 clove garlic, finely chopped

1 Heat oven to 375°. Spray roasting pan rack with cooking spray. Remove fat from pork. Mash remaining ingredients into a paste with 1/2 teaspoon of salt and 1/4 teaspoon of pepper. Rub paste on pork.

2 Place pork on rack in shallow roasting pan. Insert meat thermometer so tip is in thickest part of pork. Roast uncovered about 35 minutes or until thermometer reads 155° or when pork is slightly pink when cut into the center. Cover pork with aluminum foil and let stand 10 to 15 minutes until thermometer reads 160°.

**Betty's Tip
4 You**

Make this into a real comfort meal **with pre-made mashed potatoes and the recipe on page 178 for Baked Corn on the Cob with Herbs.**

Nutrition Information

1 SERVING: Calories 150 (Calories from Fat 45); Fat 5g (Saturated 2g); Cholesterol 70mg; Sodium 250mg; Carbohydrate 0g (Dietary Fiber 0g, Sugars 0g); Protein 26g

% Daily Value: Vitamin A 0%; Vitamin C 0%; Calcium 0%; Iron 6%
Diet Exchanges: 4 Very Lean Meat
Carbohydrate Choices: 0

Pork Tenderloin with Rosemary

1 pork tenderloin (about 3/4 pound)

1 1/2 teaspoons finely chopped rosemary or 1/2 teaspoon dried rosemary leaves, crumbled

1 clove garlic, crushed

1 Heat oven to 425°. Spray an 8-inch square baking pan with cooking spray.

2 Sprinkle 1/4 teaspoon salt and 1/8 teaspoon pepper over all sides of pork. Rub rosemary and garlic on all sides of pork. Place pork in sprayed pan.

3 Insert meat thermometer so tip is in thickest part of pork. Bake uncovered 27 to 30 minutes, or until thermometer reads 155° or pork is slightly pink when cut into the center. Cover pork with aluminum foil and let stand 10 to 15 minutes until thermometer reads 160°. Cut pork crosswise into thin slices.

Betty's Tip 4 You

When using dried rosemary, crumble the herbs in the palm of your hand to release more flavor before rubbing them onto the pork.

Nutrition Information

1 SERVING: Calories 140 (Calories from Fat 35); Fat 4g (Saturated 2g); Cholesterol 70mg; Sodium 50mg; Carbohydrate 0g (Dietary Fiber 0g, Sugars 0g); Protein 26g

% Daily Value: Vitamin A 0%; Vitamin C 0%; Calcium 0%; Iron 8%
Diet Exchanges: 4 Very Lean Meat
Carbohydrate Choices: 0

Yummy Pork Chops

4 pork loin chops, 1/2 inch thick (about 1 1/4 pounds)

3 tablespoons reduced-sodium soy sauce

3 tablespoons ketchup

2 teaspoons honey

1 Heat oven to 350°. Remove fat from pork. Place pork in ungreased square baking dish, 8 × 8 × 2 inches. Mix remaining ingredients; pour over pork.

2 Cover and bake about 45 minutes or until pork is slightly pink when cut near bone. Uncover and bake 5 minutes longer.

Betty's Tip 4 You

These Asian-inspired chops add a wonderful new dimension to everyday pork chops. Like things spicy? Substitute chili sauce or chili puree with garlic in place of the ketchup.

Nutrition Information

1 SERVING: Calories 195 (Calories from Fat 70); Fat 8g (Saturated 3g); Cholesterol 65mg; Sodium 570mg; Carbohydrate 7g (Dietary Fiber 0g, Sugars 6g); Protein 24g

% Daily Value: Vitamin A 2%; Vitamin C 0%; Calcium 0%; Iron 6%
Diet Exchanges: 1/2 Starch, 3 Very Lean Meat, 1 Fat
Carbohydrate Choices: 1/2

Slow-Cooker Scalloped Potato and Sausage Supper

1 package (5 ounces) cheesey scalloped potato with skin-on potatoes mix

1 can (10 3/4 ounces) condensed cream of mushroom with garlic soup

1 pound fully cooked kielbasa sausage, cut into 2-inch diagonal pieces

1 cup frozen green peas

1 Spray 3 1/2- to 6-quart slow cooker with cooking spray. Place uncooked potatoes in slow cooker. Mix soup, 1 soup can filled with water and Sauce Mix (from potato mix); pour over potatoes. Top with sausage.

2 Cover and cook on low heat setting 4 to 5 hours or until potatoes are tender.

3 Rinse peas with cold water to separate. Sprinkle peas over potatoes. Cover and cook on low heat setting about 5 minutes or until peas are hot.

Betty's Tip 4 You

A slow cooker is your secret when things get busy! This dish makes a great family dinner. Add a crisp green tossed salad and some long, thin, crunchy breadsticks. If you're watching the sodium and fat in your diet, use reduced-fat sausage and reduced-sodium soup in this family favorite.

Nutrition Information

1 SERVING: Calories 610 (Calories from Fat 360); Fat 40g (Saturated 14g); Cholesterol 70mg; Sodium 2400mg; Carbohydrate 43g (Dietary Fiber 4g, Sugars 7g); Protein 20g

% Daily Value: Vitamin A 8%; Vitamin C 4%; Calcium 10%; Iron 14%
Diet Exchanges: 3 Starch, 1 1/2 High-Fat Meat, 5 Fat
Carbohydrate Choices: 3

Fiesta Taco Casserole

(photo on cover)

1/2 package (13 ounces) tortilla chips, any flavor (about 4 cups)

2 cans (15 ounces each) chunky chili with beans or chili with beans

1 medium tomato, chopped (3/4 cup)

1 to 1 1/2 cups shredded Mexican cheese blend (4 to 6 ounces)

1 Heat oven to 350°. Remove 10 to 12 whole tortilla chips; set aside. Coarsely break remaining chips; place in ungreased 2-quart casserole. Top with chili. Sprinkle with tomato and cheese.

2 Bake uncovered 30 to 35 minutes or until hot and bubbly. Arrange whole tortilla chips around edge of casserole.

Betty's Tip 4 You

Set out bowls of guacamole, **sliced green onions,** chopped lettuce and sour cream. What a fun way to turn a fiesta casserole into an easy Mexican meal.

Nutrition Information

1 SERVING: Calories 460 (Calories from Fat 180); Fat 20g (Saturated 6g); Cholesterol 20mg; Sodium 1150mg; Carbohydrate 60g (Dietary Fiber 10g); Protein 19g

% Daily Value: Vitamin A 32%; Vitamin C 30%; Calcium 26%; Iron 28%
Diet Exchanges: 4 Starch, 1 High-Fat Meat, 1 Fat
Carbohydrate Choices: 4

Lamb with Creamy Mint Sauce

2/3 cup plain fat-free yogurt

1/4 cup firmly packed fresh mint leaves

2 tablespoons sugar

4 lamb loin chops, about 1 inch thick (1 pound)

1 Place yogurt, mint and sugar in blender or food processor. Cover and blend on medium speed, stopping blender occasionally to scrape sides, until leave are finely chopped.

2 Set oven control to broil. Spray broiler-pan rack with cooking spray.

3 Remove fat from lamb. Place lamb on rack in broiler pan. Broil with tops 2 to 3 inches from heat 12 to 14 minutes, turning once, until meat thermometer reads 160° (for medium doneness) or until light pink when cut near bone. Serve with mint sauce.

Betty's Tip 4 You

Would you like a bit more kick in your sauce? **Just omit the sugar and add 2 tablespoons of fresh lemon juice for a tart, delicious flavor.**

Nutrition Information

1 SERVING: Calories 170 (Calories from Fat 55); Fat 6g (Saturated 2g); Cholesterol 60mg; Sodium 75mg; Carbohydrate 9g (Dietary Fiber 0g, Sugars 9g); Protein 20g

% Daily Value: Vitamin A 4%; Vitamin C 0%; Calcium 8%; Iron 8%
Diet Exchanges: 3 Very Lean Meat, 1/2 Fruit, 1 Fat
Carbohydrate Choices: 1/2

Mustard Lamb Chops

6 lamb sirloin or shoulder
chops, about 3/4 inch thick
(about 1 1/2 pounds)

1 tablespoon chopped fresh
or 1 teaspoon dried thyme leaves

2 tablespoons Dijon mustard

1 Set oven control to broil. Remove fat from lamb. Place
lamb on rack in broiler pan. Mix remaining ingredients with
1/4 teaspoon salt. Brush half of the mustard mixture evenly
over lamb.

2 Broil lamb with tops 3 to 4 inches from heat about 4 minutes
or until brown. Turn lamb; brush with remaining mustard
mixture. Broil 5 to 7 minutes longer until meat thermometer
reads 160° for medium doneness or until light pink when cut
near bone.

Betty's Tip 4 You

Mellow your chops with different mustards,
such as honey mustard. Serve these quick-cooking
chops with buttered new potatoes with butter and steamed
green beans.

Nutrition Information

1 SERVING: Calories 155 (Calories from Fat 65); Fat 7g
(Saturated 3g); Cholesterol 70mg; Sodium 280mg;
Carbohydrate 1g (Dietary Fiber 0g, Sugars 0g); Protein 22g

% Daily Value: Vitamin A 0%; Vitamin C 0%; Calcium 0%; Iron 10%
Diet Exchanges: 3 Lean Meat
Carbohydrate Choices: 0

Honey-Glazed Chicken Breasts

6 boneless, skinless chicken breast halves (about 1 3/4 pounds)

1/2 cup orange juice

1/2 cup honey

2 tablespoons lemon juice

1 Heat oven to 375°. Grease rectangular pan, 13 × 9 × 2 inches. Place chicken in pan. Mix remaining ingredients with 1/4 teaspoon salt; pour over chicken.

2 Cover and bake 20 minutes; turn chicken. Bake uncovered 20 to 30 minutes longer or until juice of chicken is no longer pink when centers of thickest pieces are cut.

Betty's Tip 4 You

This dish has **sunny citrus flavors** that can help to chase away the winter cold. Serve the chicken with rice and a green salad with avocado and black olives. For dessert, think citrus—key lime or lemon meringue pie.

Nutrition Information

1 SERVING: Calories 210 (Calories from Fat 35); Fat 4g (Saturated 1g); Cholesterol 75mg; Sodium 170mg; Carbohydrate 17g (Dietary Fiber 0g, Sugars 17g); Protein 27g

% Daily Value: Vitamin A 0%; Vitamin C 4%; Calcium 2%; Iron 6%
Diet Exchanges: 4 Very Lean Meat, 1 Fruit
Carbohydrate Choices: 1

Chicken with Cider Glaze

2 to 2 1/2 pounds broiler-fryer chicken pieces, skin removed

1/2 cup apple cider

1/2 cup roasted-apple marinade

Chopped fresh parsley

1 Heat oven to 375°. Place chicken in ungreased rectangular pan, 13 × 9 × 2 inches. Sprinkle with 1/2 teaspoon salt and 1/4 teaspoon pepper. Pour cider and marinade over chicken.

2 Cover and bake 30 minutes; turn chicken. Bake uncovered 20 to 30 minutes longer or until juice of chicken is no longer pink when centers of thickest pieces are cut. Sprinkle with parsley.

Betty's Tip 4 You

Roasted-apple marinade is a bottled fat-free dressing and marinade made from fresh apples that have been roasted and mixed with champagne vinegar, sugar and spices. It is deep brown in color with a toasty, savory apple flavor. Look for it along with the salad dressings or marinades in your grocery store. But, if you can't find it, follow the directions above, and use applesauce instead of the marinade.

Nutrition Information

1 SERVING: Calories 330 (Calories from Fat 110); Fat 12g (Saturated 3g); Cholesterol 145mg; Sodium 440mg; Carbohydrate 9g (Dietary Fiber 0g, Sugars 7g); Protein 47g

% Daily Value: Vitamin A 0%; Vitamin C 0%; Calcium 2%; Iron 12%
Diet Exchanges: 7 Very Lean Meat, 1/2 Fruit, 1 Fat
Carbohydrate Choices: 1/2

Chicken with Cider Glaze

Crunchy Oven-Fried Chicken

1/4 cup margarine or butter

5 cups cornflakes cereal

2 teaspoons paprika

3- to 3 1/2-pound cut-up
broiler-fryer chicken

1 Heat oven to 375°. Melt margarine in jelly-roll pan,
15 1/2 × 10 1/2 × 1 inch, in oven.

2 Place cornflakes, paprika, 1 teaspoon salt and 1/4 teaspoon
pepper in blender. Cover and blend on medium speed until
mixture is fine crumbs. Dip chicken into melted margarine,
then coat evenly with cornflake mixture. Place chicken, skin
sides up, in pan.

3 Bake uncovered 45 to 60 minutes or until juice is no longer
pink when centers of thickest pieces are cut.

Betty's Tip 4 You

Here's a lower-fat alternative: **remove skin from
the chicken before dipping it into the melted margarine.** It's a great way to enjoy the taste of "fried" chicken,
without the added calories.

Nutrition Information

1 SERVING: Calories 385 (Calories from Fat 190); Fat 21g
(Saturated 5g); Cholesterol 85mg; Sodium 820mg;
Carbohydrate 21g (Dietary Fiber 1g, Sugars 2g); Protein 28g

% Daily Value: Vitamin A 30%; Vitamin C 10%; Calcium 2%; Iron 48%
Diet Exchanges: 1 1/2 Starch, 3 1/2 Medium-Fat Meat
Carbohydrate Choices: 1 1/2

Crunchy Oven-Fried Chicken

Two-Mustard Chicken

1/2 cup Dijon mustard

1/4 cup coarse-grained mustard

1/4 cup honey

8 boneless, skinless chicken breast halves (about 2 1/2 pounds)

1 Heat oven to 375°. Grease rectangular pan, 13 × 9 × 2 inches. Mix mustards and honey; spread on both sides of chicken. Place in pan.

2 Bake uncovered 25 to 35 minutes or until juice is no longer pink when centers of thickest pieces are cut.

Betty's Tip 4 You

This chicken bakes up **zesty-sweet, and is great** sprinkled with fresh thyme just before you bake it. Branch out and serve with one of the interesting varieties of winter squash that are easily available, such as butternut or acorn squash, dotted with butter and sprinkled with chives.

Nutrition Information

1 SERVING: Calories 185 (Calories from Fat 45); Fat 5g (Saturated 1g); Cholesterol 75mg; Sodium 380mg; Carbohydrate 8g (Dietary Fiber 0g, Sugars 7g); Protein 27g

% Daily Value: Vitamin A 0%; Vitamin C 0%; Calcium 2%; Iron 6%
Diet Exchanges: 12 Starch, 4 Very Lean Meat
Carbohydrate Choices: 1/2

Two-Mustard Chicken

Rosemary-Mustard Chicken

12 boneless, skinless chicken thighs (about 1 1/2 pounds)

1 tablespoon chopped fresh or 1 teaspoon dried rosemary leaves, crumbled

3 tablespoons reduced-fat sour cream

3 tablespoons Dijon mustard

1 Remove fat from chicken. Mix 1 tablespoon rosemary, 3 tablespoons sour cream, mustard and 1/4 teaspoon pepper in shallow glass or plastic dish. Add chicken; turn to coat with marinade. Cover and refrigerate at least 3 hours.

2 Heat oven to 400°. Spray rectangular pan, 13 × 9 × 2 inches, with cooking spray. Place chicken in pan. Bake uncovered about 20 minutes, or until juice of chicken is no longer pink when centers of thickest pieces are cut.

Betty's Tip
4 You

Get a jumpstart on dinner—marinate the chicken the night before, then pop it into the oven when you get home. Dinner will be ready in under half an hour!

Nutrition Information

1 SERVING: Calories 235 (Calories from Fat 110); Fat 12g (Saturated 4g); Cholesterol 90mg; Sodium 270mg; Carbohydrate 2g (Dietary Fiber 0g, Sugars 1g); Protein 30g

% Daily Value: Vitamin A 2%; Vitamin C 0%; Calcium 4%; Iron 14%
Diet Exchanges: 4 Lean Meat
Carbohydrate Choices: 0

Slow-Cooker Turkey Sausage Cassoulet

1/2 pound fully cooked smoked turkey sausage ring, cut into 1/2-inch slices

1 medium carrot, shredded (2/3 cup)

1 small onion chopped (1/4 cup)

2 cans (15 to 16 ounces each) great northern beans, drained and 3/4 cup liquid reserved

1 Mix all ingredients including reserved bean liquid with 1/4 teaspoon pepper in 2- to 3 1/2-quart slow cooker.

2 Cover and cook on low heat setting 6 to 8 hours and until flavors are blended.

Betty's Tip 4 You

This slow-cooker version of the classic French dish is hearty, and so easy. Add dried herbs—a teaspoon of marjoram or 1/4 teaspoon of thyme for extra flavor after it is cooked.

Nutrition Information

1 SERVING: Calories 350 (Calories from Fat 55); Fat 6g (Saturated 2g); Cholesterol 30mg; Sodium 580mg; Carbohydrate 58g (Dietary Fiber 15g, Sugars 3g); Protein 30g

% Daily Value: Vitamin A 56%; Vitamin C 2%; Calcium 20%; Iron 48%
Diet Exchanges: 4 Starch, 1 Very Lean Meat
Carbohydrate Choices: 4

Oriental Turkey Patties

1 pound ground turkey

1/4 cup sweet-and-sour sauce

1 can (8 ounces) water chestnuts, drained and chopped

4 medium green onions, sliced (1/4 cup)

1 Set oven control to broil. Spray broiler pan rack with cooking spray; place in broiler pan.

2 Mix turkey, sweet-and-sour sauce, water chestnuts and onions. Shape mixture into 4 patties, each about 1/2 inch thick. Place on rack in broiler pan.

3 Broil with tops about 3 inches from heat 12 to 16 minutes, turning once, until no longer pink in center.

Betty's Tip 4 You

For a lower-fat version, **use ground turkey breast, as it is made with only white meat.** Regular ground turkey contains dark meat and skin, making it higher in fat.

Nutrition Information
1 SERVING: Calories 215 (Calories from Fat 65); Fat 7g (Saturated 2g); Cholesterol 75mg; Sodium 140mg; Carbohydrate 13g (Dietary Fiber 2g, Sugars 4g); Protein 25g

% Daily Value: Vitamin A 2%; Vitamin C 4%; Calcium 4%; Iron 8%
Diet Exchanges: 3 Lean Meat, 1 Vegetable, 1/2 Fruit
Carbohydrate Choices: 1

Oriental Turkey Patties

Oven-Poached Halibut

4 halibut fillets (1 1/2 pounds),
about 1 inch thick

4 sprigs dill weed

4 slices lemon

1/4 cup dry white wine
or chicken broth

1 Heat oven to 450°. Place fish in ungreased rectangular baking dish, 11 × 7 × 1 1/2 inches. Sprinkle with 1/4 teaspoon salt and 1/8 teaspoon pepper. Place dill weed sprig and lemon slice on each. Pour wine over fish.

2 Bake uncovered 20 to 25 minutes or until fish flakes easily with fork.

Betty's Tip 4 You

Got leftovers? Toss any remaining leftovers with pasta or salad greens for another marvelous meal!

Nutrition Information

1 SERVING: Calories 150 (Calories from Fat 20); Fat 2g (Saturated 0g); Cholesterol 90mg; Sodium 320mg; Carbohydrate 0g (Dietary Fiber 0g, Sugars 0g); Protein 32g

% Daily Value: Vitamin A 0%; Vitamin C 0%; Calcium 2%; Iron 2%
Diet Exchanges: 4 1/2 Very Lean Meat
Carbohydrate Choices: 0

Chili Rice con Queso

1 package (5 ounces) salsa-style rice mix

1 1/2 cups shredded Mexican 4-cheese blend (6 ounces)

1 can (15 ounces) chili beans in sauce, undrained

1 can (14 1/2 ounces) diced tomatoes, undrained

1 Heat oven to 425°. Spray 1 1/2-quart casserole with cooking spray. Mix rice mix and 1/2 cup of the cheese in casserole.

2 Mix chili beans, tomatoes and 1/2 cup of water in 1 1/2-quart saucepan. Heat to boiling. Pour bean mixture over rice mixture in casserole; stir to mix.

3 Cover and bake 20 minutes. Sprinkle with remaining 1 cup cheese. Bake uncovered about 5 minutes or until cheese is melted and rice is tender.

Betty's Tip 4 You

Gooey cheese, canned chili beans and tomatoes, along with a salsa rice mix, make this Mexi-casserole a quick and delicious after-work dinner. If the Mexican-style cheese blend is not available, use Cheddar or Monterey Jack. This, kids will love.

Nutrition Information

1 SERVING: Calories 385 (Calories from Fat 115); Fat 13g (Saturated 8g); Cholesterol 40mg; Sodium 1620mg; Carbohydrate 51g (Dietary Fiber 6g, Sugars 5g); Protein 22g

% Daily Value: Vitamin A 22%; Vitamin C 20%; Calcium 32%; Iron 22%
Diet Exchanges: 3 Starch, 1 1/2 Medium-Fat Meat, 1 Vegetable
Carbohydrate Choices: 3 1/2

Lentil and Brown Rice Casserole

3/4 cup dried lentils (6 ounces), sorted and rinsed

1/2 cup uncooked brown rice

2 1/2 cups vegetable or chicken broth

1 bag (1 pound) frozen cut green beans or broccoli cuts

1 Heat oven to 375°. Mix lentils, rice and broth in 2-quart casserole. Cover and bake 1 hour.

2 Stir in frozen green beans. Cover and bake about 30 minutes or until liquid is absorbed and rice is tender.

Betty's Tip 4 You

The green beans are added frozen halfway through the cooking time to help maintain their bright green color and texture. The casserole is so easy, it's sure to become one of your dinner favorites. It's also great for vegetarians.

Nutrition Information

1 SERVING: Calories 135 (Calories from Fat 10); Fat 1g (Saturated 0g); Cholesterol 0mg; Sodium 430mg; Carbohydrate 31g (Dietary Fiber 8g, Sugars 3g); Protein 8g

% Daily Value: Vitamin A 14%; Vitamin C 2%; Calcium 4%; Iron 16%
Diet Exchanges: 2 Starch
Carbohydrate Choices: 2

Microwave Ravioli Casserole

1 pound ground beef

1 small onion, chopped (1/4 cup)

2 cans (15 ounces each) beef ravioli

1 cup shredded mozzarella or Cheddar cheese (4 ounces)

1 Crumble beef into 2-quart microwavable casserole. Add onion. Cover loosely and microwave on High 5 to 6 minutes, stirring after 3 minutes, until beef is no longer pink; drain.

2 Stir in ravioli. Cover tightly and microwave 5 to 7 minutes, stirring after 3 minutes, until hot. Sprinkle with cheese. Cover and let stand until cheese is melted.

Betty's Tip 4 You

Quick! This 4-ingredient Italian main dish goes together in under 20 minutes. Add some steamed broccoli and a loaf of garlic bread, and dinner is on the table in no time. For variety, try pizza- or taco-seasoned cheese instead of the mozzarella.

Nutrition Information
1 SERVING: Calories 340 (Calories from Fat 155); Fat 17g (Saturated 7g); Cholesterol 60mg; Sodium 800mg; Carbohydrate 23g (Dietary Fiber 1g, Sugars 3g); Protein 24g

% Daily Value: Vitamin A 10%; Vitamin C 10%; Calcium 14%; Iron 16%
Diet Exchanges: 1 1/2 Starch, 3 Medium-Fat Meat
Carbohydrate Choices: 1 1/2

4 Star Ideas

Great Grilling Tips

These grilling "secrets" shouldn't remain a mystery. They will save you loads of time in the long run, so check them out before heading to the grill.

★ Spray the grill with cooking spray before heating it to prevent food from sticking

★ Use long-handled barbecue tools to allow a safe distance between you and the intense heat of the grill

★ Let cooked meat rest a few minutes after removing it from the grill for heightened flavor and juicier meat, plus it is easier to carve

★ Clean the grill with a grill brush as soon as possible after using it for easier cleanup

4 Star Ideas

Burger Bar

Fire up the grill and get ready to top your burgers with these zesty sauces:

★ Use bottled barbecue sauce instead of ketchup for a quick twist on a classic sandwich

★ Put a southwestern spin on your next burger night with salsa-topped sandwiches

★ Top your burgers with pesto and Swiss cheese for a gourmet sandwich

★ Ranch dressing isn't just for salads anymore! Try it with turkey patties.

Great Grilling and Bountiful Burgers

Glazed Country Ribs   150

Grilled Southwestern Pork Chops   151

Sweet Lemon Spareribs   152

🕐 Grilled Lamb Chops   153

🕐 Grilled Steak with Parsley Pesto   154

Autumn Grilled Chicken   156

Blueberry Chicken   157

Chicken and Summer Fruit Kabobs   158

Maple- and Cranberry-Glazed Chicken   160

Peppery Horseradish Chicken   161

Pesto-Chicken Packets   162

Grilled Sesame-Ginger Turkey Slices   164

Lobster Roast   165

Grilled Salmon with Mint Marinade   166

🕐 Grilled Coney Island Burgers   167

Italian Burgers   168

Grilled Teriyaki Burgers   170

Jalapeño Burgers   171

Blue Cheese Turkey Burgers   172

Grilled Texas Turkey Burgers   174

Photos: opposite top: Autumn Grilled Chicken (page 156); opposite bottom: Blue Cheese Turkey Burgers (page 172) | 🕐 **SUPER**Express *ready in 20 minutes or less*

Glazed Country Ribs

3 pounds pork country-style ribs,
cut into serving pieces

1/2 cup orange juice

3/4 cup cocktail sauce

1/2 cup orange marmalade

1 Spray grill rack with cooking spray. Heat coals or gas grill for
direct heat.

2 While grill is heating, arrange pork, meatiest pieces to outside
edge, in 3-quart microwavable casserole. Add orange juice. Cover
and microwave on High 5 minutes. Rearrange and turn over
pork, so less-cooked pieces are to outside edge of casserole.
Cover and microwave on High 3 minutes; rearrange pork. Cover
and microwave on Medium (50%) 8 to 10 minutes or until
very little pink remains.

3 Mix cocktail sauce and marmalade; reserve 1/2 cup to serve
with pork. Drain pork; discard cooking liquid. Cover and grill
pork 5 to 6 inches from medium heat 10 to 12 minutes, turning and brushing generously with sauce mixture 2 to 3 times,
until pork is no longer pink when cut near bone.

4 Heat remaining sauce mixture to boiling; boil and stir 1 minute.
Serve with pork.

Betty's Tip 4 You

Microwave precooking means faster grilling!
Because ribs are precooked, the sweet sauce can be
added right at the beginning of grilling. Serve with coleslaw and
Zesty Salsa Corn on page 180 for a fantastic dinner.

Nutrition Information
1 SERVING: Calories 540 (Calories from Fat 200); Fat 22g
(Saturated 8g); Cholesterol 115mg; Sodium 690mg;
Carbohydrate 45g (Dietary Fiber 1g, Sugars 36g); Protein 40g

% Daily Value: Vitamin A 12%; Vitamin C 18%; Calcium 2%; Iron 10%
Diet Exchanges: 1 Starch, 5 Lean Meat, 2 Fruit, 1 1/2 Fat
Carbohydrate Choices: 3

Grilled Southwestern Pork Chops

8 pork loin or rib chops, about
1/2 inch thick (about 2 pounds)

1 tablespoon chili powder

1 teaspoon ground cumin

1 large clove garlic, finely chopped

1 Remove excess fat from pork. Mix remaining ingredients with
1/4 teaspoon of pepper and 1/4 teaspoon of salt; rub evenly on
both sides of pork. Cover and refrigerate 1 hour to blend flavors.

2 Heat coals or gas grill for direct heat. Cover and grill pork 4 to
6 inches from medium heat 10 to 12 minutes, turning frequently, until thermometer reads 160° or until pork is slightly
pink when cut near bone.

Betty's Tip
4 You

Want to spice things up? Use cayenne pepper
instead of black pepper on the pork chops. Add
sprigs of fresh cilantro and red chilies to the serving platter for
even more spice.

Nutrition Information

1 SERVING: Calories 130 (Calories from Fat 55); Fat 6g
(Saturated 2g); Cholesterol 50mg; Sodium 115mg;
Carbohydrate 1g (Dietary Fiber 0g, Sugars 0g); Protein 18g

% Daily Value: Vitamin A 6%; Vitamin C 0%; Calcium 0%; Iron 4%
Diet Exchanges: 2 1/2 Lean Meat
Carbohydrate Choices: 0

Sweet Lemon Spareribs

6 pounds pork spareribs, cut into serving pieces

1 can (6 ounces) frozen lemonade concentrate, thawed

3/4 cup barbecue sauce

1 Place pork in Dutch oven. Add enough water to cover pork. Heat to boiling; reduce heat to low. Cover and simmer about 1 1/2 hours or until tender.

2 Remove pork to rectangular 13 × 9 × 2-inch baking dish. Mix lemonade concentrate and barbecue sauce. Pour over pork; turn pork to coat with marinade. Cover and refrigerate, turning pork occasionally, at least 4 hours but no longer than 24 hours.

3 Spray grill rack with cooking spray. Heat coals or gas grill for direct heat.

4 Remove pork from marinade; reserve marinade. Grill pork, meaty sides up, uncovered, 4 inches from medium-hot heat about 30 minutes, turning and brushing frequently with marinade, until glazed and heated through. Discard any remaining marinade.

Betty's Tip 4 You

These spareribs make great finger food as well, and are terrific served as an appetizer for a party. You can cook them a day ahead, then put the ribs on the grill to wam them up just before the party.

Nutrition Information

1 SERVING: Calories 790 (Calories from Fat 485); Fat 54g (Saturated 20g); Cholesterol 215mg; Sodium 440mg; Carbohydrate 24g (Dietary Fiber 0g, Sugars 20g); Protein 52g

% Daily Value: Vitamin A 2%; Vitamin C 4%; Calcium 8%; Iron 20%
Diet Exchanges: 1/2 Starch, 7 Medium-Fat Meat, 1 Fruit
Carbohydrate Choices: 1 1/2

Grilled Lamb Chops

SUPER
Express

2 cups mint-flavored apple jelly

8 cloves garlic, crushed

8 loin, rib or shoulder lamb chops,
1 inch thick

1 Spray grill rack with cooking spray. Heat coals or gas grill for
direct heat.

2 Heat apple jelly and garlic with 2 tablespoons of water over
medium heat, stirring constantly, until jelly is melted.

3 Remove fell (the paper-like covering) if it is on chops. Slash
outer edge of fat on lamb chops diagonally at 1-inch intervals
to prevent curling (do not cut into the meat).

4 Cover and grill lamb 3 to 4 inches from medium heat 9 to 11
minutes, turning and brushing 2 to 3 times with the sauce,
until thermometer reads 160° or lamb is light pink when cut
near the bone for medium doneness.

5 Heat remaining sauce to boiling; boil 1 minute. Serve lamb
with sauce.

Betty's Tip
4 You

If you prefer broiling to grilling, **prepare lamb chops
as directed above. Set oven control to broil. Place
lamb on rack in broiler pan; place broiler pan so tops of 3/4- to
1-inch thick chops are 2 to 3 inches from heat, 1- to 2-inch thick
chops are 3 to 5 inches from heat. Broil until brown. The chops
should be about half done.**

Sprinkle brown side with salt and pepper if desired. Turn chops;
broil until brown.

Nutrition Information

1 SERVING: Calories 670 (Calories from Fat 110); Fat 12g
(Saturated 4g); Cholesterol 115mg; Sodium 135mg;
Carbohydrate 105g (Dietary Fiber 2g, Sugars 75g); Protein 36g

% Daily Value: Vitamin A 0%; Vitamin C 12%; Calcium 4%; Iron 20%
Diet Exchanges: 5 Very Lean Meat, 7 Fruit, 2 Fat
Carbohydrate Choices: 7

SUPER *Express*

Grilled Steak with Parsley Pesto

1/2 cup chopped fresh parsley

1/4 cup olive or vegetable oil

4 cloves garlic, cut into pieces

4 beef T-bone steaks, about 1 inch thick (about 8 ounces each)

1 Heat coals or gas grill for direct heat. Place parsley, oil and garlic in food processor or blender. Cover and process until smooth.

2 Cut outer edge of fat on beef diagonally at 1-inch intervals to prevent curling (do not cut into beef).

3 Cover and grill beef 3 to 4 inches from medium heat, 5 minutes for medium-rare or 7 minutes for medium, brushing frequently with parsley mixture. Turn; brush generously with parsley mixture. Grill 5 to 7 minutes or longer until thermometer reads 145° for medium-rare or 160° for medium doneness. Sprinkle with 1 teaspoon salt and 1/2 teaspoon pepper. Discard any remaining parsley mixture.

Betty's Tip 4 You

Want a juicy steak? Use tongs or a spatula when handling the steaks during grilling, instead of a fork, so you don't pierce the beef and allow the juices to cook out.

Nutrition Information
1 SERVING: Calories 330 (Calories from Fat 205); Fat 23g (Saturated 6g); Cholesterol 75mg; Sodium 660mg; Carbohydrate 1g (Dietary Fiber 0g, Sugars 0); Protein 30g

% Daily Value: Vitamin A 14%; Vitamin C 8%; Calcium 2%; Iron 16%
Diet Exchanges: 4 Medium-Fat Meat, 1 Fat
Carbohydrate Choices: 0

Grilled Steak with Parsley Pesto

Autumn Grilled Chicken

1 pound cut-up boneless, skinless chicken breast for stir-fry

2 large firm ripe pears, sliced

1 large cooking apple, sliced

1/2 cup roasted-apple vinaigrette or malt vinegar

1 Heat coals or gas grill for direct heat.

2 Place chicken, pears and apple on one side of each of 4 sheets of heavy-duty aluminum foil, 18 × 12 inches. Top with vinaigrette and 1/2 teaspoon of salt. Fold other half of foil over chicken and fruit so edges meet. Seal edges, making a tight 1/2-inch fold; fold again. Allow space on sides for circulation and expansion. Repeat folding to seal each side.

3 Cover and grill packets 4 to 5 inches from medium heat 10 to 15 minutes or until chicken is no longer pink in center. Place foil packets on plates. To serve, cut a large X across top of packet; fold foil back.

Betty's Tip 4 You

Sage adds wonderful flavor to this fruity chicken. When you assemble the packets for the grill, divide 2 tablespoons of chopped fresh sage among the packets. There are different varieties of sage you might want to try such as purple or pineapple sage.

Nutrition Information
1 SERVING: Calories 285 (Calories from Fat 100); Fat 11g (Saturated 3g); Cholesterol 70mg; Sodium 360mg; Carbohydrate 26g (Dietary Fiber 4g, Sugars 20g); Protein 20g

% Daily Value: Vitamin A 2%; Vitamin C 6%; Calcium 2%; Iron 8%
Diet Exchanges: 3 Lean Meat, 2 Fruit
Carbohydrate Choices: 2

Blueberry Chicken

4 boneless, skinless chicken breast halves (about 1 1/4 pounds)

1/2 cup blueberry jam

2 tablespoons white vinegar

1 cup fresh or frozen (thawed and drained) blueberries

1 Spray grill rack with cooking spray. Heat coals or gas grill for direct heat.

2 Sprinkle chicken with 1/4 teaspoon salt. Mix jam and vinegar.

3 Cover and grill 4 to 6 inches from medium heat 10 minutes; turn chicken. Cover and grill 10 to 15 minutes longer, brushing with jam mixture, until juice of chicken is no longer pink when centers of thickest pieces are cut. Discard any remaining jam mixture. Serve chicken with blueberries.

Betty's Tip 4 You

Be adventurous—use your blueberries in this unusual dish. Continue the adventure by serving the chicken on a bed of couscous mixed with mixed dried fruit and cashews.

Nutrition Information

1 SERVING: Calories 275 (Calories from Fat 35); Fat 4g (Saturated 1g); Cholesterol 75mg; Sodium 80mg; Carbohydrate 33g (Dietary Fiber 1g, Sugars 23g); Protein 27g

% Daily Value: Vitamin A 0%; Vitamin C 6%; Calcium 2%; Iron 6%
Diet Exchanges: 4 Very Lean Meat, 2 Fruit
Carbohydrate Choices: 2

Chicken and Summer Fruit Kabobs

1 pound boneless, skinless chicken breasts, cut into 1 1/2-inch pieces

2 medium peaches or nectarines, cut into 1-inch wedges

2 medium plums, cut into 1-inch wedges

1/2 cup peach or apricot jam

1 Spray grill rack with cooking spray. Heat coals or gas grill for direct heat.

2 Thread chicken, peaches and plums alternately on each of six 10- to 12-inch metal skewers, leaving space between each piece. Mix jam with 1/2 teaspoon of salt.

3 Cover and grill kabobs 4 to 5 inches from medium heat 15 to 20 minutes, turning occasionally and brushing with jam, until chicken is no longer pink in center.

Betty's Tip 4 You

For an even more colorful dish, **use different colored plums, such as red and purple, and different types of peaches, such as yellow or white.**

Nutrition Information

1 SERVING: Calories 195 (Calories from Fat 25); Fat 3g (Saturated 1g); Cholesterol 45mg; Sodium 250mg; Carbohydrate 25g (Dietary Fiber 1g, Sugars 18g); Protein 17g

% Daily Value: Vitamin A 2%; Vitamin C 4%; Calcium 2%; Iron 4%
Diet Exchanges: 2 1/2 Very Lean Meat, 1 1/2 Fruit, 1/2 Fat
Carbohydrate Choices: 1 1/2

Chicken and Summer Fruit Kabobs

Maple- and Cranberry-Glazed Chicken

1 can (16 ounces) whole berry cranberry sauce

1/2 cup maple-flavored syrup

6 boneless, skinless chicken breast halves

1 Spray grill rack with cooking spray. Heat coals or gas grill for direct heat.

2 Mix half of the cranberry sauce with syrup. Sprinkle 1/2 teaspoon of salt over chicken.

3 Cover and grill chicken 4 to 5 inches from medium heat 10 minutes; turn chicken. Grill 10 to 15 minutes longer, brushing occasionally with cranberry mixture, until juice of chicken is no longer pink when centers of thickest pieces are cut.

4 Heat remaining cranberry sauce to boiling. Boil 1 minute. Serve with remaining cranberry sauce.

Betty's Tip 4 You

Leftovers? This glazed chicken makes a great addition to stir-fries. Just cut up the chicken and add to the skillet during the last 5 minutes of cooking time.

Nutrition Information

1 SERVING: Calories 340 (Calories from Fat 35); Fat 4g (Saturated 1g); Cholesterol 75mg; Sodium 310mg; Carbohydrate 49g (Dietary Fiber 1g, Sugars 37g); Protein 27g

% Daily Value: Vitamin A 0%; Vitamin C 0%; Calcium 2%; Iron 6%
Diet Exchanges: 3 Very Lean Meat, 3 Fruit, 1 Fat
Carbohydrate Choices: 3

Peppery Horseradish Chicken

1/4 cup prepared horseradish

1/4 cup sour cream

3- to 3 1/2-pound cut-up broiler-fryer chicken

1 Spray grill rack with cooking spray. Heat coals or gas grill for direct heat.

2 Mix horseradish, sour cream and 1/4 teaspoon of pepper.

3 Place chicken, skin sides up, on grill; brush with horseradish mixture. Cover and grill 5 to 6 inches from medium heat 15 minutes. Turn chicken; brush with horseradish mixture. Cover and grill 20 to 40 minutes longer, turning and brushing with horseradish mixture occasionally, until juice of chicken is no longer pink when centers of thickest pieces are cut. Discard any remaining horseradish mixture.

Betty's Tip 4 You

A perfect choice for a picnic, this chicken is great paired with Zesty Salsa Corn on page 180. Tuck some deli potato salad in the cooler and take an assortment of fresh fruit for an easy, no-fuss meal.

Nutrition Information

1 SERVING: Calories 245 (Calories from Fat 135); Fat 15g (Saturated 5g); Cholesterol 90mg; Sodium 110mg; Carbohydrate 1g (Dietary Fiber 0g, Sugars 1g); Protein 27g

% Daily Value: Vitamin A 2%; Vitamin C 0%; Calcium 2%; Iron 6%
Diet Exchanges: 4 Lean Meat, 1/2 Fat
Carbohydrate Choices: 0

Pesto-Chicken Packets

4 boneless, skinless chicken breast halves (about 1 1/4 pounds)

8 roma (plum) tomatoes, cut into 1/2-inch slices

4 small zucchini, cut into 1/2-inch slices

1/2 cup prepared basil pesto

1 Heat coals or gas grill for direct heat.

2 Place 1 chicken breast half, 2 sliced tomatoes and 1 sliced zucchini on 1 side of each of 4 sheets of heavy-duty aluminum foil, 18 × 12 inches. Spoon 2 tablespoons pesto over chicken mixture. Fold other half of foil over chicken and vegetables so edges meet. Seal edges, making a tight 1 1/2-inch fold; fold again. Allow space on sides for circulation and expansion. Repeat folding to seal each side.

3 Cover and grill packets 4 to 5 inches from medium heat 20 to 25 minutes, or until juice of chicken is no longer pink when centers of thickest pieces are cut. Place foil packets on plates. To serve, cut a large X across top of packet; fold back foil.

Betty's Tip
4 You

No time to mind the grill? **Bake the packets in a 350° oven for 25 to 30 minutes instead.** Try using foil bags for easier prep.

Nutrition Information

1 SERVING: Calories 355 (Calories from Fat 190); Fat 21g (Saturated 4g); Cholesterol 80mg; Sodium 350mg; Carbohydrate 10g (Dietary Fiber 3g, Sugars 4g); Protein 32g

% Daily Value: Vitamin A 36%; Vitamin C 26%; Calcium 16%; Iron 14%
Diet Exchanges: 4 Medium-Fat Meat, 2 Vegetable
Carbohydrate Choices: 1/2

Pesto-Chicken Packets

Grilled Sesame-Ginger Turkey Slices

2 tablespoons teriyaki sauce

1 tablespoon sesame seed, toasted

1 teaspoon ground ginger

1 pound uncooked turkey breast slices, about 1/4 inch thick

1 Spray grill rack with cooking spray. Heat coals or gas grill for direct heat. Mix teriyaki sauce, sesame seed and ginger.

2 Cover and grill turkey 4 to 6 inches from medium heat 15 to 20 minutes, brushing frequently with sauce mixture and turning after 10 minutes, until turkey is no longer pink in center. Discard any remaining sauce mixture.

Betty's Tip 4 You

Serve on a bed of hot-cooked **Japanese curly noodles** or hot cooked rice, and garnish with sliced green onions. Steamed snow peas go well with the turkey, and for dessert try ginger ice cream. Can't find it? You can add chopped candied ginger to vanilla ice cream, or just enjoy the vanilla ice cream by itself.

Nutrition Information

1 SERVING: Calories 140 (Calories from Fat 20); Fat 2g (Saturated 0g); Cholesterol 75mg; Sodium 410mg; Carbohydrate 2g (Dietary Fiber 0g, Sugars 1g); Protein 27g

% Daily Value: Vitamin A 0%; Vitamin C 0%; Calcium 2%; Iron 10%
Diet Exchanges: 4 Very Lean Meat
Carbohydrate Choices: 0

Lobster Roast

4 live lobsters (each 1 to 1 1/4 pounds)

1/2 cup margarine or butter, melted

1 lemon, cut into wedges

1 loaf French bread, sliced

1 Carefully cut each lobster lengthwise in half with sharp knife or poultry shears. Remove the dark vein that runs through the center of the body and the stomach, which is just behind the head. Leave the green liver and the coral roe, which are delicacies.

2 Spray grill rack with cooking spray. Heat coals or gas grill for direct heat.

3 Brush lobster meat generously with margarine. Place lobster halves, shell sides down, on grill. Grill uncovered about 4 inches from medium-hot heat 10 to 15 minutes, brushing frequently with margarine, until meat turns white. Don't turn during grilling or you'll lose the juices that collect in the shell.

4 Serve lobsters hot with lemon wedges, additional melted margarine and French bread.

Betty's Tip 4 You

Live lobsters can be found in tanks in many supermarket fish sections, and in most fish stores. They taste terrific and are a festive change on the grill. If you'd prefer not to cut into a live lobster, parboil it in enough boiling water to cover for 5 to 10 minutes, and then cut in half.

Nutrition Information

1 SERVING: Calories 605 (Calories from Fat 245); Fat 27g (Saturated 5g); Cholesterol 75mg; Sodium 1360mg; Carbohydrate 58g (Dietary Fiber 3g, Sugars 1g); Protein 32g

% Daily Value: Vitamin A 30%; Vitamin C 0%; Calcium 16%; Iron 20%
Diet Exchanges: 4 Starch, 3 Lean Meat, 3 Fat
Carbohydrate Choices: 4

Grilled Salmon with Mint Marinade

4 small salmon, tuna or swordfish steaks, 3/4 inch thick (about 1 1/2 pounds)

1/2 cup chopped fresh mint leaves

1/4 cup olive oil

3 tablespoons fresh lemon juice

1 Place salmon steaks in ungreased rectangular baking dish, 11 × 7 × 1 1/2 inches. Beat remaining ingredients with 1/2 teaspoon salt and 1/2 teaspoon pepper with wire whisk until blended. Pour over fish. Cover and refrigerate at least 1 hour but no longer than 24 hours, turning fish occasionally.

2 Spray grill rack with cooking spray. Heat coals or gas grill for direct heat. Remove fish from marinade; reserve marinade. Grill fish uncovered about 4 inches from medium-high heat 5 minutes, brushing frequently with marinade. Turn carefully; brush generously with marinade. Grill 5 to 10 minutes longer until fish flakes easily with fork.

3 Heat remaining marinade to boiling. Boil 1 minute. Serve marinade with fish.

Betty's Tip 4 You

You can also cook the salmon in a skillet, if you prefer. Marinate as directed and place in skillet. Cook on one side over medium heat until light brown, about 5 minutes. Turn the fish over, and continue cooking 4 to 6 minutes longer until fish flakes easily with fork.

Nutrition Information

1 SERVING: Calories 355 (Calories from Fat 205); Fat 23g (Saturated 5g); Cholesterol 110mg; Sodium 400mg; Carbohydrate 1g (Dietary Fiber 0g, Sugars 0g); Protein 36g

% Daily Value: Vitamin A 12%; Vitamin C 4%; Calcium 2%; Iron 8%
Diet Exchanges: 5 Lean Meat, 2 Fat
Carbohydrate Choices: 0

Grilled Coney Island Burgers

1 pound ground beef

1 can (7 1/2 ounces) chili
with beans

1 tablespoon chopped green chilies

6 frankfurter buns, split and
warmed

1 Spray grill rack with cooking spray. Heat coals or gas grill for direct heat.

2 Shape ground beef into 6 rolls, each about 5 inches long and 3/4 inch thick. Mix chili and green chilies in small grill pan; heat on grill until hot.

3 Grill ground beef rolls about 4 inches from medium coals, turning once, until desired doneness, 3 to 5 minutes on each side for medium. Serve in frankfurter buns; spoon about 2 tablespoons chili mixture into each bun.

Betty's Tip 4 You

Prefer to broil the burgers? Mix chili with beans and green chilies in saucepan; heat until hot. Prepare ground beef rolls as directed above. Set oven control to broil. Place rolls on rack in broiler pan. Broil with tops about 3 inches from heat, turning once, until desired doneness, about 3 minutes on each side for medium. Serve as directed above.

Nutrition Information

1 SERVING: Calories 295 (Calories from Fat 115); Fat 13g (Saturated 5g); Cholesterol 45mg; Sodium 390mg; Carbohydrate 26g (Dietary Fiber 2g, Sugars 6g); Protein 19g

% Daily Value: Vitamin A 4%; Vitamin C 4%; Calcium 8%; Iron 16%
Diet Exchanges: 2 Starch, 2 Medium-Fat Meat
Carbohydrate Choices: 2

Italian Burgers

1 pound ground turkey

1/3 cup spaghetti sauce

3 tablespoons finely chopped onion

4 slices (1 ounce each) provolone cheese

1 Spray grill rack with cooking spray. Heat coals or gas grill for direct heat.

2 Mix turkey, spaghetti sauce and onion. Shape mixture into 4 patties, each about 3/4 inch thick.

3 Cover and grill patties 4 to 6 inches from medium heat 14 to 16 minutes, turning once, until no longer pink in center and juice is clear. About 1 minute before burgers are done, top each with cheese slice. Grill until cheese is melted.

Betty's Tip 4 You

Remember this recipe **when you are looking for something different.** Serve with slices of tomato and lettuce, and top with sliced olives for the flavors of Italy in a burger.

Nutrition Information

1 SERVING: Calories 290 (Calories from Fat 135); Fat 15g (Saturated 7g); Cholesterol 100mg; Sodium 450mg; Carbohydrate 5g (Dietary Fiber 0g, Sugars 2g); Protein 32g

% Daily Value: Vitamin A 8%; Vitamin C 2%; Calcium 22%; Iron 6%
Diet Exchanges: 4 Lean Meat, 1 Vegetable, 1 Fat
Carbohydrate Choices: 0

Italian Burgers

Grilled Teriyaki Burgers

1 pound ground beef

2 tablespoons soy sauce

1/4 teaspoon crushed gingerroot
or 1/8 teaspoon ground ginger

1 clove garlic, crushed

1 Shape ground beef into 4 patties, each about 3/4 inch thick. Mix remaining ingredients; spoon onto patties. Turn patties; cover and refrigerate 10 minutes.

2 Spray grill rack with cooking spray. Heat coals or gas grill for direct heat. Grill patties about 4 inches from medium coals, turning once, until desired doneness, 5 to 7 minutes on each side for medium.

Betty's Tip
4 You

You can also use the broiler for these patties. Prepare the patties as directed above and set the oven control to broil. Place patties on rack in broiler pan. Broil with tops about 3 inches from heat, turning once, until desired doneness, about 5 minutes on each side for medium.

Nutrition Information
1 SERVING: Calories 230 (Calories from Fat 145); Fat 16g (Saturated 6g); Cholesterol 65mg; Sodium 510mg; Carbohydrate 1g (Dietary Fiber 0g, Sugars 0g); Protein 21g

% Daily Value: Vitamin A 2%; Vitamin C 0%; Calcium 0%; Iron 10%
Diet Exchanges: 3 Medium-Fat Meat
Carbohydrate Choices: 0

Jalapeño Burgers

1 1/2 pounds lean ground beef or ground buffalo

1 medium onion, finely chopped (1/2 cup)

2 to 3 jalapeño chilies, seeded and finely chopped

1 clove garlic, finely chopped

1 Spray grill rack with cooking spray. Heat coals or gas grill for direct heat.

2 Mix all ingredients. Shape mixture into 6 patties, about 1/2 inch thick.

3 Grill patties uncovered about 4 inches from medium heat 8 to 12 minutes, turning once, until no longer pink in center and juice is clear.

Betty's Tip 4 You

To continue the Mexican theme, serve these spunky burgers in flour tortillas accompanied by tomato salsa, taco sauce or chili sauce and topped with slices of Monterey Jack cheese.

Nutrition Information
1 SERVING: Calories 210 (Calories from Fat 145); Fat 16g (Saturated 6g); Cholesterol 65mg; Sodium 65mg; Carbohydrate 2g (Dietary Fiber 0g, Sugars 1g); Protein 21g

% Daily Value: Vitamin A 2%; Vitamin C 2%; Calcium 0%; Iron 10%
Diet Exchanges: 3 Lean Meat, 1 Fat
Carbohydrate Choices: 0

Blue Cheese Turkey Burgers

1 1/2 pounds ground turkey

1/4 cup mayonnaise or salad dressing

4 ounces crumbled blue cheese

1 large red onion, sliced

1 Spray grill rack with cooking spray. Heat coals or gas grill for direct heat.

2 Mix turkey, mayonnaise and blue cheese. Shape mixture into 6 patties, about 3/4 inch thick.

3 Cover and grill patties 4 to 5 inches from medium heat 15 to 20 minutes, turning once, until turkey is no longer pink. Top with red onion slices.

Betty's Tip 4 You

Make this flavorful burger into a sandwich **and serve it on a hamburger bun. Toasted buns always add extra flavor**—to toast buns, grill cut sides down about 4 minutes or until golden brown.

Nutrition Information

1 SERVING: Calories 290 (Calories from Fat 170); Fat 19g (Saturated 6g); Cholesterol 95mg; Sodium 390mg; Carbohydrate 1g (Dietary Fiber 0g, Sugars 1g); Protein 29g

% Daily Value: Vitamin A 2%; Vitamin C 0%; Calcium 10%; Iron 6%
Diet Exchanges: 4 Medium-Fat Meat
Carbohydrate Choices: 0

Blue Cheese Turkey Burgers

Grilled Texas Turkey Burgers

1 pound ground turkey

1/3 cup barbecue sauce

1 can (4 ounces) chopped green chilies, drained

4 slices (1 ounce each) Monterey Jack cheese with jalapeño peppers

1 Spray grill rack with cooking spray. Heat coals or gas grill for direct heat.

2 Mix turkey, barbecue sauce and chilies. Shape mixture into 4 patties, each about 3/4 inch thick.

3 Cover and grill patties 4 to 6 inches from medium heat 14 to 16 minutes, turning once, until no longer pink. About 1 minute before burgers are done, top each with cheese slice. Grill until cheese is melted.

Betty's Tip 4 You

Turn up the heat by using 2 or 3 chopped fresh jalapeño chilies instead of the canned chilies. And, if you'd prefer a sandwich, serve the burgers on hamburger buns or grilled Texas toast.

Nutrition Information

1 SERVING: Calories 300 (Calories from Fat 135); Fat 15g (Saturated 7g); Cholesterol 105mg; Sodium 570mg; Carbohydrate 9g (Dietary Fiber 1g, Sugars 7g); Protein 32g

% Daily Value: Vitamin A 10%; Vitamin C 8%; Calcium 22%; Iron 10%
Diet Exchanges: 1/2 Starch, 4 Lean Meat, 1 Fat
Carbohydrate Choices: 1/2

Grilled Texas Turkey Burgers

4 Star Ideas

Microwave Magic

Microwave your vegetables for a speedy side:

★ Put fresh green beans sprinkled with salt, pepper and olive oil in a shallow dish, cover with plastic wrap and microwave on High for 3 to 4 minutes.

★ Place baby carrots in a microwavable dish with salt, sesame seed, margarine and a touch of water. Microwave on High 2 to 3 minutes until crisp-tender.

★ Layer sliced zucchini in a casserole dish with Italian dressing and Italian herb seasoning. Microwave on High 6 to 8 minutes.

★ Arrange sliced tomato on a plate sprinkled with salt and pepper, bread crumbs and shredded cheese. Microwave on High 3 minutes.

4 Star Ideas

Meal in a Potato

Turn your side into a main course with these easy toppers for your microwaved "baked" potato: Microwave a potato that has been pricked with a fork on High for 4 to 5 minutes, turning potato over after 2 minutes, until tender. Let stand uncovered 5 minutes.

★ Canned shrimp, cream cheese and chives

★ Tuna salad from the deli and ranch dressing

★ Hot cooked chopped broccoli and teriyaki sauce

★ Sour cream, salsa and finely chopped green onions

7

Round-Out-Your-Meal Savory Sides

Baked Corn on the Cob with Herbs   178

Zesty Salsa Corn   180

Dilled Carrots and Pea Pods   181

Honey-Glazed Carrots   182

Leeks with Rosemary-Garlic Butter   183

Roasted Vegetables   184

Slow-Cooker Spicy Black-Eyed Peas   185

Stir-Fried Green Beans and Peppers   186

Horseradish Mashed Potatoes   188

Parsley Potatoes   190

Roasted Red Potatoes   192

Slow-Cooker Scalloped Potatoes   193

Sweet Potato Slices   194

Twice-Baked Potatoes   195

Photos: opposite top: Dilled Carrots and Pea Pods (page 181); opposite bottom: Horseradish Mashed Potatoes (page 188)

SUPER*Express* *ready in 20 minutes or less*

Baked Corn on the Cob with Herbs

4 ears corn

20 to 24 sprigs fresh basil, rosemary, thyme, dill weed, marjoram or sage

1 Heat oven to 450°. Husk and remove silk from corn. Place each ear on 12-inch square of aluminum foil. Spray on all sides with cooking spray. Sprinkle with 1/4 teaspoon of salt and 1/8 teaspoon of pepper. Place 5 to 6 sprigs of fresh herb around each ear. Seal foil.

2 Place sealed ears of corn directly on oven rack. Bake about 20 minutes or until corn is tender.

Betty's Tip 4 You

For a tantalizing blend of flavors, team two herbs together with the corn—basil and rosemary, or thyme and dill weed are especially good combinations. Serve with plenty of melted butter to drizzle over the top.

Nutrition Information

1 SERVING: Calories 110 (Calories from Fat 10); Fat 1g (Saturated 0g); Cholesterol 0mg; Sodium 610mg; Carbohydrate 25g (Dietary Fiber 3g, Sugars 3g); Protein 3g

% Daily Value: Vitamin A 4%; Vitamin C 4%; Calcium 0%; Iron 2%
Diet Exchanges: 1 Starch, 1/2 Other Carbohydrate
Carbohydrate Choices: 1 1/2

Baked Corn on the Cob with Herbs

SUPER *Express*

Zesty Salsa Corn

1 bag (1 pound) frozen whole kernel corn

1/2 cup salsa

1/4 cup sliced ripe olives

1 Cook corn as directed on package.

2 Stir in salsa and olives; cook until hot.

Betty's Tip 4 You

Salsa is a great boon to those trying to watch their waistlines; it not only tastes great, but is low in calories and low-fat. This salsa adds zip, not calories, to plain cooked fish or chicken.

Nutrition Information

1 SERVING: Calories 100 (Calories from Fat 10); Fat 1g (Saturated 0g); Cholesterol 0mg; Sodium 180mg; Carbohydrate 19g (Dietary Fiber 3g, Sugars 2g); Protein 3g

% Daily Value: Vitamin A 6%; Vitamin C 10%; Calcium 2%; Iron 4%
Diet Exchanges: 1 Starch
Carbohydrate Choices: 1

Dilled Carrots and Pea Pods

SUPER
Express

1 1/2 cups baby-cut carrots

1 1/2 cups snow (Chinese)
pea pods (about 5 ounces),
strings removed

1 tablespoon margarine or butter

2 teaspoons chopped fresh
or 1/2 teaspoon dried dill weed

1 Place carrots in 1 inch of water in 2-quart saucepan. Heat
to boiling over high heat; reduce heat to low. Cover and
simmer about 4 minutes or until carrots are crisp-tender.
Do not drain water.

2 Add pea pods to carrots in saucepan. Heat uncovered to
boiling; boil 2 to 3 minutes, stirring occasionally, until pea
pods are crisp-tender. Be careful not to overcook the pea pods.
Drain carrots and pea pods , return to saucepan.

3 Stir margarine, dill weed and 1/8 teaspoon salt into carrots and
pea pods until margarine is melted.

Betty's Tip
4 You

To save time use one 6-ounce package of frozen
snow (Chinese) pea pods to substitute for the fresh
pea pods. Thaw them before adding to the carrots.

Nutrition Information

1 SERVING: Calories 55 (Calories from Fat 25); Fat 3g
(Saturated 1g); Cholesterol 0mg; Sodium 55mg;
Carbohydrate 6g (Dietary Fiber 2g, Sugars 3g); Protein 1g

% Daily Value: Vitamin A 100%; Vitamin C 12%; Calcium 2%; Iron 4%
Diet Exchanges: 1 Vegetable, 1/2 Fat
Carbohydrate Choices: 1/2

Honey-Glazed Carrots

1 bag (1 pound) baby-cut carrots

2 tablespoons honey

1 tablespoon margarine or butter

Ground nutmeg, if desired

1 Place carrots in 1 inch of water in 2-quart saucepan. Heat to boiling; reduce heat to low. Cover and simmer 10 to 15 minutes or until tender. Drain well.

2 Add honey and margarine to carrots in saucepan. Cook carrots, stirring frequently, until margarine is melted and carrots are glazed. Sprinkle with nutmeg.

Betty's Tip 4 You

These yummy carrots are a hit with kids—try them with Honey-Glazed Chicken Breasts on page 133. Add another flavor dimension to this veggie side dish by stirring in a teaspoon of finely chopped gingerroot and a teaspoon of grated orange peel.

Nutrition Information

1 SERVING: Calories 80 (Calories from Fat 20); Fat 2g (Saturated 0g); Cholesterol 0mg; Sodium 50mg; Carbohydrate 14g (Dietary Fiber 2g, Sugars 10g); Protein 1g

% Daily Value: Vitamin A 100%; Vitamin C 6%; Calcium 2%; Iron 2% **Diet Exchanges:** 1 Vegetable, 1/2 Other Carbohydrate, 1/2 Fat **Carbohydrate Choices:** 1

Leeks with Rosemary-Garlic Butter

2 tablespoons margarine or butter, softened

1 teaspoon chopped fresh or 1/4 teaspoon dried rosemary leaves, crushed

1 clove garlic, finely chopped

6 small leeks (about 1 1/2 pounds)

1 Spray grill rack with cooking spray. Heat coals or gas grill for direct heat.

2 Mix margarine, rosemary and garlic.

3 Remove green tops of leeks to within 2 inches of white part. Cut leeks lengthwise in half to within 1 inch of root end. Wash leeks several times in water; drain.

4 Cover and grill leeks 4 to 6 inches from medium heat 15 to 20 minutes, turning and brushing occasionally with margarine mixture, until tender and light brown.

Betty's Tip 4 You

When you're looking for leeks, choose those that have crisp, bright green tops and blemish-free white bulbs.

Nutrition Information

1 SERVING: Calories 55 (Calories from Fat 35); Fat 4g (Saturated 2g); Cholesterol 10mg; Sodium 35mg; Carbohydrate 4g (Dietary Fiber 1g, Sugars 2g); Protein 1g

% Daily Value: Vitamin A 8%; Vitamin C 8%; Calcium 4%; Iron 4%
Diet Exchanges: 1 Vegetable, 1/2 Fat
Carbohydrate Choices: 0

Roasted Vegetables

1 medium red or green bell pepper, cut into 8 strips

1/2 medium onion, cut into 4 wedges

1 medium zucchini, cut into 1-inch pieces

1/4 pound whole mushrooms

1 Heat the oven to 425°. Spray the bottom of a 13 × 9-inch rectangular baking pan with cooking spray. Arrange the vegetables in a single layer in the sprayed pan. Spray the vegetables with cooking spray until lightly coated. Sprinkle with 1/4 teaspoon salt and 1/8 teaspoon pepper.

2 Bake uncovered 15 minutes. Remove the pan from the oven. Turn vegetables over. Bake uncovered about 10 minutes longer or until vegetables are crisp-tender when pierced with a fork.

Betty's Tip 4 You

Got leftovers? Sprinkle leftover veggies on a sauce-topped pizza crust. Top with shredded mozzarella cheese, and bake until the cheese melts. Yum!

Nutrition Information

1 SERVING: Calories 35 (Calories from Fat 0); Fat 0g (Saturated 0g); Cholesterol 0mg; Sodium 150mg; Carbohydrate 7g (Dietary Fiber 2g, Sugars 4g); Protein 2g

% Daily Value: Vitamin A 42%; Vitamin C 52%; Calcium 2%; Iron 4%
Diet Exchanges: 1 1/2 Vegetable
Carbohydrate Choices: 1/2

Slow-Cooker Spicy Black-Eyed Peas

1 pound dried black-eyed peas (2 cups), sorted and rinsed

1 medium onion, chopped (1/2 cup)

3/4 cup salsa

1 Mix peas and onion with 6 cups of water, 1 teaspoon of salt and 1/2 teaspoon of pepper in 3 1/2- to 6-quart slow cooker.

2 Cover and cook on high heat setting 3 to 4 hours or until peas are tender. Stir in salsa.

3 Cover and cook on high heat setting about 10 minutes or until hot.

Betty's Tip 4 You

The extra flavor of hot salsa goes so well with black-eyed peas, but use whichever salsa suits your family's taste—mild, medium or hot. The salsa is added after the peas are tender because sometimes the acid in the tomatoes prevent the peas from becoming tender.

Nutrition Information

1 SERVING: Calories 165 (Calories from Fat 10); Fat 1g (Saturated 0g); Cholesterol 0mg; Sodium 110mg; Carbohydrate 35g (Dietary Fiber 10g, Sugars 4g); Protein 13g

% Daily Value: Vitamin A 4%; Vitamin C 4%; Calcium 4%; Iron 22%
Diet Exchanges: 2 Starch, 1 Vegetable
Carbohydrate Choices: 2

SUPER *Express*

Stir-Fried Green Beans and Peppers

1/2 pound green beans, cut crosswise in half

1 medium yellow or red bell pepper, cut into 1/2-inch pieces

1 tablespoon vegetable oil

2 teaspoons chopped fresh or 1/2 teaspoon dried marjoram leaves

1 Heat 1/4 cup of water and beans to boiling in a 10-inch skillet over high heat. Reduce heat. Cover and simmer about 5 minutes or until beans are crisp-tender.

2 Add bell pepper and oil to the beans in the skillet. Increase heat to medium-high. Stir-fry about 2 minutes, until bell pepper is crisp-tender. Stir in marjoram.

Betty's Tip *4 You*

It's important to drain off any remaining water from the skillet after cooking the beans to keep the stir-fry crisp. For ease, pour beans into a strainer or colander and then return them to the skillet.

Nutrition Information

1 SERVING: Calories 55 (Calories from Fat 35); Fat 4g (Saturated 1g); Cholesterol 0mg; Sodium 5mg; Carbohydrate 5g (Dietary Fiber 2g, Sugars 3g); Protein 1g

% Daily Value: Vitamin A 8%; Vitamin C 46%; Calcium 2%; Iron 2%
Diet Exchanges: 1 Vegetable, 1/2 Fat
Carbohydrate Choices: 0

Stir-Fried Green Beans and Peppers

Horseradish Mashed Potatoes

4 medium unpeeled potatoes (about 1 1/2 pounds), cut into 1/2-inch slices

1/3 cup plain fat-free yogurt

1 tablespoon prepared horseradish

2 to 4 tablespoons fat-free (skim) milk

1 Heat 1 inch of water to boiling in 3-quart saucepan. Add potatoes. Heat to boiling; reduce heat to low. Simmer uncovered about 15 minutes or until tender; drain. Return potatoes to saucepan. Shake pan with potatoes over low heat to dry; remove from heat.

2 Mash potatoes until no lumps remain. Beat in yogurt, horseradish and 1/2 teaspoon salt. Add milk in small amounts, beating after each addition (amount of milk needed to make potatoes smooth and fluffy depends on the kind of potatoes used). Beat vigorously until potatoes are light and fluffy.

Betty's Tip 4 You

If you're not a fan of horseradish go ahead and leave it out. The potatoes will still be heavenly! Sprinkle with fresh chopped parsley for an added touch of flavor.

Nutrition Information

1 SERVING: Calories 140 (Calories from Fat 0); Fat 0g (Saturated 0g); Cholesterol 0mg; Sodium 340mg; Carbohydrate 31g (Dietary Fiber 2g, Sugars 3g); Protein 4g

% Daily Value: Vitamin A 0%; Vitamin C 12%; Calcium 6%; Iron 8%
Diet Exchanges: 1 Starch, 1 Other Carbohydrate
Carbohydrate Choices: 2

Horseradish Mashed Potatoes

Parsley Potatoes

10 to 12 new potatoes
(about 1 1/2 pounds)

2 tablespoons margarine
or butter, melted

1 tablespoon chopped parsley

1 Add 1 inch of water to a Dutch oven. Cover and heat to boiling over high heat. Add potatoes. Cover and heat to boiling, reduce heat. Cook covered 20 to 25 minutes or until tender; drain and return to Dutch oven.

2 Drizzle margarine over potatoes, sprinkle with parsley, 1/4 teaspoon salt and 1/8 teaspoon pepper. Stir gently to coat potatoes.

Betty's Tip 4 You

Pressed for time? Microwave the potatoes. Choose potatoes of similar size. Pierce potatoes with a fork to allow steam to escape. Place potatoes and 1/4 cup water in a 2-quart microwavable casserole, arranging larger potatoes to the outside edge. Cover with plastic wrap, folding back 2-inch edge to vent. Microwave on High 10 to 12 minutes, stirring after 5 minutes, until tender when pierced with a fork. Let stand covered 1 minute; drain in a strainer. Melt margarine and continue with the recipe.

Nutrition Information

1 SERVING: Calories 165 (Calories from Fat 55); Fat 6g (Saturated 1g); Cholesterol 0mg; Sodium 230mg; Carbohydrate 25g (Dietary Fiber 2g, Sugars 1g); Protein 2g

% Daily Value: Vitamin A 8%; Vitamin C 10%; Calcium 0%; Iron 8%
Diet Exchanges: 1 Starch, 1/2 Other Carbohydrate, 1 Fat
Carbohydrate Choices: 1 1/2

Parsley Potatoes

Roasted Red Potatoes

12 small red potatoes (about 1 1/2 pounds)

2 tablespoons olive or vegetable oil

2 medium green onions, sliced

2 tablespoons chopped fresh or 2 teaspoons dried rosemary leaves, crumbled

1 Heat the oven to 350°.

2 Place the potatoes in ungreased 8- or 9-inch square or 13 × 9-inch rectangular baking pan. Drizzle oil over potatoes, and turn potatoes so all sides are coated.

3 Sprinkle the onions and rosemary over the potatoes; stir.

4 Bake uncovered about 1 hour 15 minutes, stirring occasionally, until potatoes are tender.

Betty's Tip 4 You

Most small red potatoes are about 2 inches in diameter. If they are much bigger, cut them in half so they will be more tender in about 1 hour.

Nutrition Information

1 SERVING: Calories 215 (Calories from Fat 65); Fat 7g (Saturated 1g); Cholesterol 0mg; Sodium 10mg; Carbohydrate 35g (Dietary Fiber 4g, Sugars 2g); Protein 3g

% Daily Value: Vitamin A 2%; Vitamin C 16%; Calcium 2%; Iron 10%
Diet Exchanges: 1 Starch, 1 Other Carbohydrate, 1 1/2 Fat
Carbohydrate Choices: 2

Slow-Cooker Scalloped Potatoes

6 medium potatoes (2 pounds), cut into 1/8-inch slices

1 can (10 3/4 ounces) condensed cream of onion soup

1 can (5 ounces) evaporated milk (2/3 cup)

1 jar (2 ounces) diced pimientos, undrained

1 Spray inside of 3 1/2- to 6-quart slow cooker with cooking spray.

2 Mix all ingredients with 1/2 teaspoon salt and 1/4 teaspoon pepper; pour into cooker.

3 Cover and cook on low heat setting 10 to 12 hours or until potatoes are tender.

Betty's Tip 4 You

Vary the taste of these creamy potatoes by using whatever cream soup you have on hand, such as cream of mushroom, chicken or broccoli. You may want to add a thinly sliced small onion or 1/4 teaspoon onion powder if you decide not to use the onion soup.

Nutrition Information

1 SERVING: Calories 155 (Calories from Fat 25); Fat 3g (Saturated 1g); Cholesterol 10mg; Sodium 0mg; Carbohydrate 28g (Dietary Fiber 2g, sugars 5g); Protein 4g

% Daily Value: Vitamin A 6%; Vitamin C 14%; Calcium 10%; Iron 8%
Diet Exchanges: 1 Starch, 1 Other Carbohydrate, 1/2 Fat
Carbohydrate Choices: 2

Sweet Potato Slices

3 pounds sweet potatoes or yams

1/3 cup margarine or butter, melted

1/3 cup coconut, toasted

1 Spray grill rack with cooking spray. Heat coals or gas grill for direct heat.

2 Peel sweet potatoes; cut into 1/2-inch diagonal slices. Heat 1 inch of water to boiling in 3-quart saucepan. Add sweet potatoes. Cover and heat to boiling; reduce heat to low. Simmer about 12 minutes or until almost tender; drain. Mix margarine and 1/2 teaspoon salt.

3 Grill sweet potato slices uncovered 4 inches from medium heat about 20 minutes, brushing frequently with margarine mixture and turning once.

4 To serve, sprinkle sweet potatoes with coconut.

Betty's Tip 4 You

It's not just a side dish! **Turn these luscious grilled sweet potato slices into dessert by adding a scoop of ice cream for a great new taste.**

Nutrition Information

1 SERVING: Calories 265 (Calories from Fat 110); Fat 12g (Saturated 3g); Cholesterol 0mg; Sodium 160mg; Carbohydrate 36g (Dietary Fiber 4g, Sugars 22g); Protein 3g

% Daily Value: Vitamin A 100%; Vitamin C 28%; Calcium 4%; Iron 4%
Diet Exchanges: 1 1/2 Starch, 1 Fruit, 2 Fat
Carbohydrate Choices: 2 1/2

Twice-Baked Potatoes

2 large baking potatoes (russet or Idaho), 8 to 10 ounces each

2 to 4 tablespoons milk

2 tablespoons margarine or butter, softened

1/2 cup shredded Cheddar cheese (2 ounces)

1 Heat the oven to 375°. Pierce the potatoes on all sides with a fork to allow steam to escape. Place potatoes directly on the oven rack. Bake 1 hour to 1 hour 15 minutes or until potatoes are tender.

2 When potatoes are cool enough to handle, cut them lengthwise in half. Scoop out the insides into a medium bowl, leaving about 1/4-inch shell in the potato skin.

3 Increase the temperature of the oven to 400°.

4 Mash the potatoes with a potato masher or electric mixer until no lumps remain. Add the milk in small amounts, beating after each addition. The amount of milk needed to make potatoes smooth and fluffy depends on the type of potato used.

5 Add the margarine, 1/8 teaspoon salt and a dash pepper. Beat vigorously until potatoes are light and fluffy. Stir in the cheese. Fill the potato shells with the mashed potato mixture. Place on an ungreased cookie sheet. Bake potatoes uncovered about 20 minutes or until hot.

Betty's Tip 4 You

You can make these potatoes and freeze them for up to 2 months. Just defrost them in the refrigerator. Then bake them uncovered on an ungreased cookie sheet at 400° for about 40 minutes or until hot.

Nutrition Information

1 SERVING: Calories 185 (Calories from Fat 100); Fat 11g (Saturated 4g); Cholesterol 15mg; Sodium 250mg; Carbohydrate 16g (Dietary Fiber 1g, Sugars 1g); Protein 5g

% Daily Value: Vitamin A 8%; Vitamin C 6%; Calcium 8%; Iron 2%
Diet Exchanges: 1 Starch, 2 Fat
Carbohydrate Choices: 1

4 Star Ideas

Fruitful Desserts

Create a new dessert sensation with fruit salad from the deli:

★ Toss with honey, lime juice and slivered almonds for a thirst-quenching treat

★ Add sour cream, honey and orange juice for a quick summer cool-off

★ Add a splash of orange juice, a dash of sugar and chopped fresh mint for a cool, refreshing flavor

★ Combine sweet fruit with salty bacon bits for a great hit that's easy to fix

4 Star Ideas

Easy Sundae Toppers and Pound Cake Dippers

Make simple desserts special! Jazz up your desserts with these easy ideas:

★ Drizzle honey and sprinkle instant coffee granules over your cake or ice cream

★ Try a pound cake dipper of fruit-flavored yogurt

★ Mix chocolate syrup into whipped cream for a sundae topper

★ Stir sliced strawberries and lemon juice into cherry pie filling for a pound cake topper

Finishing Dinner with Delectable Desserts

Creamy Raspberry-Filled Angel Cake   198

Easy Fruit Crisp "Dump" Dessert   200

Pears with Raspberry Sauce   201

Strawberries with Marsala Sauce   202

Strawberries Romanoff   204

Munchy Chocolate Cookies   205

Old-Fashioned Peanut Butter Cookies   206

Cantaloupe Sorbet   208

Cherry Ribbon Cake Slices   209

Frozen Chocolate Mousse   210

Creamy Frozen Apricot Bars   212

Honey Sundaes   213

Lemon Ice   214

Pineapple Ice   215

Photos: opposite top: Pears with Raspberry Sauce
(page 201); opposite bottom: Creamy Raspberry-Filled
Angel Cake (page 198)

SUPER*Express* *ready in 20 minutes or less*

Creamy Raspberry-Filled Angel Cake

1 package (4-serving size) sugar-free raspberry-flavored gelatin

1 pint (2 cups) raspberries

1 container (8 ounces) frozen fat-free whipped topping, thawed

1 round (10 inches in diameter) angel food cake

1 Pour 1 cup of boiling water over gelatin in large bowl; stir until gelatin is dissolved. Stir in 1/2 cup of cold water. Refrigerate about 1 hour or until thickened but not set.

2 Fold 1 pint raspberries and half of the whipped topping into gelatin mixture. Refrigerate about 15 minutes or until thickened but not set.

3 Split cake horizontally to make 3 layers. (To split, mark side of cake with toothpicks and cut with long, thin serrated knife.) Fill layers with gelatin mixture. Spoon or pipe remaining whipped topping onto top of cake.

Betty's Tip 4 You

For a fun cake with kid appeal, use confetti angel food cake and decorate with candy sprinkles or colored sugar. And for those strawberry lovers, use strawberry-flavored gelatin and 2 cups chopped strawberries for the raspberries.

Nutrition Information
1 SERVING: Calories 190 (Calories from Fat 10); Fat 1g (Saturated 0g); Cholesterol 0mg; Sodium 400mg; Carbohydrate 41g (Dietary Fiber 2g, Sugars 30g); Protein 4g

% Daily Value: Vitamin A 0%; Vitamin C 8%; Calcium 0%; Iron 4%
Diet Exchanges: 1 Starch, 2 Fruit
Carbohydrate Choices: 3

Creamy Raspberry-Filled Angel Cake

Easy Fruit Crisp "Dump" Dessert

1 can (21 ounces) cherry pie filling

1 can (8 ounces) crushed pineapple, undrained

1 package (1 pound 2.25 ounces) yellow cake mix with pudding

1/2 cup margarine or butter, melted

1 Heat oven to 350°. Spread pie filling and pineapple in ungreased rectangular pan, 13 × 9 × 2 inches. Stir cake mix (dry) and margarine in large bowl, using spoon, until crumbly. Sprinkle mixture evenly over fruit.

2 Bake 45 to 50 minutes or until deep golden brown. Cool 30 minutes. Serve warm or cool.

Betty's Tip 4 You

The name of this dessert implies fun—children of all ages will enjoy making and eating it. Make it even better by serving it with ice cream or sweetened whipped cream.

Nutrition Information

1 SERVING: Calories 315 (Calories from Fat 110); Fat 12g (Saturated 2g); Cholesterol 0mg; Sodium 400mg; Carbohydrate 50g (Dietary Fiber 1g, Sugars 39g); Protein 2g

% Daily Value: Vitamin A 8%; Vitamin C 2%; Calcium 6%; Iron 4%
Diet Exchanges: 1 Starch, 2 Fruit, 2 Fat
Carbohydrate Choices: 3

Pears with Raspberry Sauce

3 large, firm pears (about 1 1/2 pounds)

1 tablespoon vegetable oil

1 package (10 ounces) frozen raspberries in syrup, thawed

1 teaspoon lemon juice

1 Heat coals or gas grill for direct heat.

2 Peel pears; cut lengthwise in half and remove cores. Lightly brush both sides with oil.

3 Cover and grill pears, cut sides up, 4 to 6 inches from medium heat 5 minutes; turn. Cover and grill about 5 minutes longer or until tender.

4 While pears are grilling, place raspberries and lemon juice in blender or food processor. Cover and blend on medium speed, stopping blender occasionally to scrape sides, or process about 30 seconds, until well blended. Strain raspberry mixture to remove seeds, if desired.

5 Serve hot pears with raspberry sauce.

Betty's Tip 4 You

Enjoy a "pear-fectly" delicious fruit dessert cooked on the grill. Drizzle it with hot fudge sauce for a special touch. Double the recipe! Plan on serving extra pears with a spoonful of yogurt for a breakfast bonus.

Nutrition Information

1 SERVING: Calories 145 (Calories from Fat 25); Fat 3g (Saturated 0g); Cholesterol 0mg; Sodium 0mg; Carbohydrate 28g (Dietary Fiber 5g, Sugars 21g); Protein 1g

% Daily Value: Vitamin A 0%; Vitamin C 10%; Calcium 2%; Iron 2%
Diet Exchanges: 2 Fruit, 1/2 Fat
Carbohydrate Choices: 2

Strawberries with Marsala Sauce

4 cups (2 pints) strawberries

2 cups sweet Marsala wine

1/2 cup sugar

6 egg yolks

1 Remove stems from strawberries. Arrange strawberries, stem ends down, in shallow serving dish, about 10 inches in diameter. Pour 1 cup of wine over strawberries.

2 Pour just enough water into bottom of double boiler so that top of double boiler does not touch water. Heat water over medium heat (do not boil).

3 Meanwhile, beat sugar and egg yolks in top of double boiler, using wire whisk, until pale yellow and slightly thickened. Place top of double boiler over bottom. Gradually beat remaining 1 cup wine into egg yolk mixture. Cook, beating constantly, until mixture thickens and coats wire whisk and thermometer reads 160° (do not boil).

4 Pour sauce over strawberries. Serve immediately.

Betty's Tip 4 You

There really is no exact substitute for Marsala wine, but if you want to try another sweet wine, an Eiswein or a Riesling is a good substitute.

Nutrition Information

1 SERVING: Calories 275 (Calories from Fat 125); Fat 14g (Saturated 2g); Cholesterol 210mg; Sodium 15mg; Carbohydrate 33g (Dietary Fiber 2g, Sugars 26g); Protein 4g

% Daily Value: Vitamin A 6%; Vitamin C 96%; Calcium 4%; Iron 6%
Diet Exchanges: 1 Starch, 1 Fruit, 3 Fat
Carbohydrate Choices: 2

Strawberries with Marsala Sauce

Strawberries Romanoff

1 quart strawberries, cut into halves

1/2 cup powdered sugar

3 to 4 tablespoons kirsch or orange-flavored liqueur or orange juice

1 cup chilled whipping (heavy) cream

1 Reserve 6 strawberry halves for garnish. Sprinkle remaining halves with powdered sugar and kirsch; toss. Cover and refrigerate 2 hours.

2 Just before serving, beat whipping cream in chilled medium bowl until soft peaks form; fold in strawberries. Garnish each serving with reserved strawberry half.

Betty's Tip 4 You

Try using tangy blueberries and raspberries. They add taste, color and texture to this simple yet very elegant recipe.

Nutrition Information

1 SERVING: Calories 205 (Calories from Fat 115); Fat 13g (Saturated 8g); Cholesterol 45mg; Sodium 15mg; Carbohydrate 21g (Dietary Fiber 2g, Sugars 19g); Protein 1g

% Daily Value: Vitamin A 8%; Vitamin C 96%; Calcium 4%; Iron 2%
Diet Exchanges: 1 1/2 Fruit, 2 1/2 Fat
Carbohydrate Choices: 1 1/2

Munchy Chocolate Cookies

1 package (1 pound 2.25 ounces) devil's food cake mix with pudding

1/3 cup vegetable oil

2 eggs

Granulated sugar

1 Heat oven to 350°. Mix cake mix (dry), oil and eggs in large bowl with spoon until dough forms (some dry mix will remain).

2 Shape dough into 1-inch balls; roll in sugar. Place about 2 inches apart on ungreased cookie sheet.

3 Bake 8 to 10 minutes or until set. Remove from cookie sheet to wire rack.

Betty's Tip
4 You

The tops of these cookies look crinkled, **and have a soft, chewy texture.** Turn them into kissed crinkles by pressing a milk chocolate kiss or white chocolate kiss with milk chocolate stripes into the center of each cookie immediately after removing them from the oven.

Nutrition Information

1 COOKIE: Calories 75 (Calories from Fat 25); Fat 3g (Saturated 0g); Cholesterol 10mg; Sodium 100mg; Carbohydrate 11g (Dietary Fiber 0g, Sugars 8g); Protein 1g

% Daily Value: Vitamin A 0%; Vitamin C 0%; Calcium 2%; Iron 2%
Diet Exchanges: 1 Other Carbohydrate, 1/2 Fat
Carbohydrate Choices: 1

Old-Fashioned Peanut Butter Cookies

1 package (1 pound 2.25 ounces) yellow cake mix with pudding

1 cup creamy peanut butter

2 eggs

1/4 cup granulated sugar

1 Heat oven to 375°. Beat half of the cake mix (dry), 1/3 cup of water, peanut butter and eggs in large bowl with electric mixer on medium speed until smooth, or mix with spoon. Stir in remaining cake mix.

2 Drop dough by rounded teaspoonfuls about 2 inches apart onto ungreased cookie sheet. Flatten in crisscross pattern with fork dipped in sugar.

3 Bake 10 to 12 minutes or until golden brown. Cool 1 minute; remove from cookie sheet to wire rack.

Betty's Tip 4 You

Love the combination of chocolate and peanut butter? Make chocolate peanut butter sandwich cookies by spreading 1 to 2 teaspoons of chocolate frosting between a pair of cookies.

Nutrition Information

1 COOKIE: Calories 85 (Calories from Fat 35); Fat 3g (Saturated 1g); Cholesterol 10mg; Sodium 90mg; Carbohydrate 10g (Dietary Fiber 0g, Sugars 7g); Protein 2g

% Daily Value: Vitamin A 0%; Vitamin C 0%; Calcium 0%; Iron 0%
Diet Exchanges: 1/2 Starch, 1 Fat
Carbohydrate Choices: 1/2

Old-Fashioned Peanut Butter Cookies

Cantaloupe Sorbet

1 medium cantaloupe, peeled and cut into 1-inch pieces (6 cups)

2 tablespoons sugar

2 tablespoons lemon juice

Fresh mint leaves

1 Place cantaloupe, sugar and lemon juice in blender or food processor. Cover and blend on high speed, stopping occasionally to scrape sides, until uniform consistency. Pour into square pan, 9 × 9 × 2 inches. Cover and freeze 1 to 1 1/2 hours or until partially frozen.

2 Spoon partially frozen mixture into blender or food processor. Cover and blend on high speed until smooth. Pour into pan. Cover and freeze about 2 hours or until firm. (Or pour into 1-quart ice-cream freezer; freeze according to manufacturer's directions.)

3 Let stand 10 minutes at room temperature before spooning into dessert dishes. Garnish with mint leaves.

Betty's Tip
4 You

Serve this refreshingly delicious sorbet in hollowed-out cantaloupe halves, or even tall margarita glasses. Cut fun cactus shapes from the cantaloupe rind to stick into the sorbet for a fun touch.

Nutrition Information

1 SERVING: Calories 50 (Calories from Fat 0); Fat 0g (Saturated 0g); Cholesterol 0mg; Sodium 10mg; Carbohydrate 12g (Dietary Fiber 1g, Sugars 12g); Protein 1g

% Daily Value: Vitamin A 48%; Vitamin C 66%; Calcium 0%; Iron 0%
Diet Exchanges: 1 Fruit
Carbohydrate Choices: 1

Cherry Ribbon Cake Slices

1 prepared angel food loaf cake (about 7 1/2 × 4 inches)

1 pint chocolate or French vanilla ice cream, slightly softened

1 can (21 ounces) sweet cherry pie filling

2 tablespoons crème de cassis or kirsch

1 Carefully split cake horizontally to make 2 layers.

2 Spread ice cream over bottom layer; place top layer on ice cream. Wrap and freeze until firm, at least 4 hours.

3 Heat cherry filling until warm; stir in crème de cassis. Cut filled cake into slices. Spoon warm cherry filling over each slice.

Betty's Tip 4 You

A dollop of **cherry yogurt** mixed with whipped topping gives these tasty slices a special finish. Add a drizzle of chocolate to make this colorful dessert extra special.

Nutrition Information
1 SERVING: Calories 255 (Calories from Fat 35); Fat 4g (Saturated 2g); Cholesterol 10mg; Sodium 300mg; Carbohydrate 51g (Dietary Fiber 1g, Sugars 41g); Protein 4g

% Daily Value: Vitamin A 2%; Vitamin C 2%; Calcium 4%; Iron 4%
Diet Exchanges: 1 Starch, 2 1/2 Fruit, 1/2 Fat
Carbohydrate Choices: 3 1/2

Frozen Chocolate Mousse

2 cups whipping (heavy) cream

1/4 cup almond-, chocolate- or coffee-flavored liqueur or Italian syrup

1/2 cup chocolate-flavored syrup

Crushed cookies or chopped nuts, if desired

1 Beat the whipping cream in a chilled large bowl with the electric mixer on high speed until stiff peaks form.

2 Gently pour the liqueur and chocolate syrup over the whipped cream. To fold ingredients together, use a rubber spatula to cut down vertically through the whipped cream, then slide the spatula across the bottom of the bowl and up the side, turning the whipped cream over. Rotate the bowl one-quarter turn, and repeat this down-across-up motion. Continue mixing in this way just until ingredients are blended.

3 Spread whipped cream mixture into a 9-inch square ungreased pan.

4 Cover and freeze at least 4 hours but no longer than 2 months. Cut mousse into squares. Garnish with crushed cookies. Serve immediately. Cover and freeze any remaining mousse.

Betty's Tip 4 You

The whipping cream will beat up more easily if the bowl and mixer beater are chilled in the refrigerator for about 20 minutes before beating.

Nutrition Information
1 SERVING: Calories 245 (Calories from Fat 170); Fat 19g (Saturated 12g); Cholesterol 65mg; Sodium 35mg; Carbohydrate 16g (Dietary Fiber 0g, Sugars 12g); Protein 2g

% Daily Value: Vitamin A 12%; Vitamin C 0%; Calcium 4%; Iron 2%
Diet Exchanges: 1 Starch, 4 Fat
Carbohydrate Choices: 1

Frozen Chocolate Mousse

Creamy Frozen Apricot Bars

1 cup vanilla fat-free yogurt

1/2 cup apricot spreadable fruit

1 package (8 ounces) reduced-fat cream cheese (Neufchâtel), cubed

1 Line square pan, 8 × 8 × 2 inches, with plastic wrap. Place all ingredients in blender or food processor. Cover and blend on high speed, stopping occasionally to scrape sides, until smooth. Carefully spread in pan. Cover and freeze about 2 hours or until firm.

2 Remove frozen mixture from pan, using plastic wrap to lift. Cut into 4 squares; make 2 crisscross cuts in each square to form 4 triangles.

Betty's Tip 4 You

Be as creative as you like when combining flavors of yogurt and fruit. How about frozen strawberry-banana or lemon-raspberry bars? Go for it!

Nutrition Information
1 SERVING: Calories 65 (Calories from Fat 25); Fat 3g (Saturated 2g); Cholesterol 10mg; Sodium 65mg; Carbohydrate 8g (Dietary Fiber 1g, Sugars 7g); Protein 2g

% Daily Value: Vitamin A 4%; Vitamin C 2%; Calcium 2%; Iron 0%
Diet Exchanges: 1/2 Starch, 1/2 Fat
Carbohydrate Choices: 1/2

Honey Sundaes

4 cups chocolate chip ice cream

1/2 cup honey

1/4 cup apricot brandy

2 teaspoons uncooked ground coffee

1 Scoop 1 cup of ice cream into each of 4 dessert dishes.

2 Mix honey and brandy. Spoon over ice cream; sprinkle each with 1/2 teaspoon ground coffee.

Betty's Tip 4 You

Try different ice creams for other tasty flavors like chocolate, coffee or vanilla. For a surprise flavor and texture, sprinkle each serving with uncooked coffee grounds.

Nutrition Information

1 SERVING: Calories 440 (Calories from Fat 135); Fat 15g (Saturated 9g); Cholesterol 60mg; Sodium 110mg; Carbohydrate 71g (Dietary Fiber 0g, Sugars 61g); Protein 5g

% Daily Values: Vitamin A 10%; Vitamin C 2%; Calcium 16%; Iron 2%
Diet Exchanges: 1/2 Milk, 4 Other Carbohydrate, 3 1/2 Fat
Carbohydrate Choices: 5

Lemon Ice

1 cup sugar

1 tablespoon grated lemon peel

1 cup fresh lemon juice

1 Heat 2 cups of water and sugar to boiling in 2-quart saucepan; reduce heat. Simmer uncovered 5 minutes; remove from heat. Stir in lemon peel and lemon juice. Cool 10 minutes.

2 Freeze in ice-cream maker as directed by manufacturer. Or cool to room temperature, then pour into ungreased loaf pan, 9 × 5 × 3 inches, and freeze 1 1/2 to 2 hours or until mushy in center. Stir mixture; freeze about 1 hour longer, stirring every 30 minutes, until firm.

3 Cut into 1/2-inch chunks and place in serving bowl. Cover and freeze until ready to serve.

Betty's Tip
4 You

Traditionally served between courses **as a** "palate refresher," lemon ice is also the perfect ending to a great meal. It's wonderful on its own, but you can also add a drizzle of chocolate sauce, if you like.

Nutrition Information

1 SERVING: Calories 110 (Calories from Fat 0); Fat 0g (Saturated 0g); Cholesterol 0mg; Sodium 5mg; Carbohydrate 27g (Dietary Fiber 0g, Sugars 26g); Protein 0g

% Daily Value: Vitamin A 0%; Vitamin C 12%; Calcium 0%; Iron 0%
Diet Exchanges: 2 Fruit
Carbohydrate Choices: 2

Pineapple Ice

1 medium pineapple, cut into
1-inch pieces (4 cups)

1/2 cup light corn syrup

2 tablespoons lemon juice

1 Place all ingredients in blender or food processor. Cover and blend on high speed, stopping occasionally to scrape sides, until smooth. Pour into loaf pan, 9 × 5 × 3 inches. Cover and freeze about 2 hours or until firm around edges but soft in center.

2 Spoon partially frozen mixture into blender or food processor. Cover and blend on high speed until smooth. Pour back into pan. Cover and freeze about 3 hours or until firm. (Or pour into 1-quart ice-cream freezer; freeze according to manufacturer's directions.)

3 Let stand 10 minutes at room temperature before spooning into dessert dishes.

Betty's Tip 4 You

Save yourself from chopping! Look for precut pineapple chunks, usually available in the produce section of your supermarket. Next time, you might want to try cantaloupe or watermelon for a fun flavor twist.

Nutrition Information

1 SERVING: Calories 90 (Calories from Fat 0); Fat 0g (Saturated 0g); Cholesterol 0mg; Sodium 25mg; Carbohydrate 23g (Dietary Fiber 1g, Sugars 13g); Protein 0g

% Daily Value: Vitamin A 0%; Vitamin C 16%; Calcium 0%; Iron 0%
Diet Exchanges: 1 1/2 Fruit
Carbohydrate Choices: 1 1/2

Helpful Nutrition and Cooking Information

Nutrition Guidelines

We provide nutrition information for each recipe that includes calories, fat, cholesterol, sodium, carbohydrate, fiber and protein. Individual food choices can be based on this information.

Criteria Used for Calculating Nutrition Information

- The first ingredient was used wherever a choice is given (such as 1/3 cup sour cream or plain yogurt).
- The first ingredient amount was used wherever a range is given (such as 3- to 3 1/2–pound cut-up broiler-fryer chicken).
- The first serving number was used wherever a range is given (such as 4 to 6 servings).
- "If desired" ingredients and recipe variations were not included (such as sprinkle with brown sugar, if desired).
- Only the amount of a marinade or frying oil that is estimated to be absorbed by the food during preparation or cooking was calculated.

Ingredients Used in Recipe Testing and Nutrition Calculations

- Ingredients used for testing represent those that the majority of consumers use in their homes: large eggs, 2% milk, 80%-lean ground beef, canned ready-to-use chicken broth and vegetable oil spread containing not less than 65 percent fat.
- Fat-free, low-fat or low-sodium products were not used, unless otherwise indicated.
- Solid vegetable shortening (not butter, margarine, nonstick cooking sprays or vegetable oil spread as they can cause sticking problems) was used to grease pans, unless otherwise indicated.

Equipment Used in Recipe Testing

We use equipment for testing that the majority of consumers use in their homes. If a specific piece of equipment (such as a wire whisk) is necessary for recipe success, it is listed in the recipe.

- Cookware and bakeware without nonstick coatings were used, unless otherwise indicated.
- No dark-colored, black or insulated bakeware was used.
- When a pan is specified in a recipe, a metal pan was used; a baking dish or pie plate means ovenproof glass was used.
- An electric hand mixer was used for mixing only when mixer speeds are specified in the recipe directions. When a mixer speed is not given, a spoon or fork was used.

Cooking Terms Glossary

Beat: Mix ingredients vigorously with spoon, fork, wire whisk, hand beater or electric mixer until smooth and uniform.

Boil: Heat liquid until bubbles rise continuously and break on the surface and steam is given off. For rolling boil, the bubbles form rapidly.

Chop: Cut into coarse or fine irregular pieces with a knife, food chopper, blender or food processor.

Cube: Cut into squares 1/2 inch or larger.

Dice: Cut into squares smaller than 1/2 inch.

Grate: Cut into tiny particles using small rough holes of grater (citrus peel or chocolate).

Grease: Rub the inside surface of a pan with shortening, using pastry brush, piece of waxed paper or paper towel, to prevent food from sticking during baking (as for some casseroles).

Julienne: Cut into thin, matchlike strips, using knife or food processor (vegetables, fruits, meats).

Mix: Combine ingredients in any way that distributes them evenly.

Sauté: Cook foods in hot oil or margarine over medium-high heat with frequent tossing and turning motion.

Shred: Cut into long thin pieces by rubbing food across the holes of a shredder, as for cheese, or by using a knife to slice very thinly, as for cabbage.

Simmer: Cook in liquid just below the boiling point on top of the stove; usually after reducing heat from a boil. Bubbles will rise slowly and break just below the surface.

Stir: Mix ingredients until uniform consistency. Stir once in a while for stirring occasionally, often for stirring frequently and continuously for stirring constantly.

Toss: Tumble ingredients (such as green salad) lightly with a lifting motion, usually to coat evenly or mix with another food.

Metric Conversion Chart

Volume

U.S. Units	Canadian Metric	Australian Metric
1/4 teaspoon	1 mL	1 ml
1/2 teaspoon	2 mL	2 ml
1 teaspoon	5 mL	5 ml
1 tablespoon	15 mL	20 ml
1/4 cup	50 mL	60 ml
1/3 cup	75 mL	80 ml
1/2 cup	125 mL	125 ml
2/3 cup	150 mL	170 ml
3/4 cup	175 mL	190 ml
1 cup	250 mL	250 ml
1 quart	1 liter	1 liter
1 1/2 quarts	1.5 liters	1.5 liters
2 quarts	2 liters	2 liters
2 1/2 quarts	2.5 liters	2.5 liters
3 quarts	3 liters	3 liters
4 quarts	4 liters	4 liters

Measurements

Inches	Centimeters
1	2.5
2	5.0
3	7.5
4	10.0
5	12.5
6	15.0
7	17.5
8	20.5
9	23.0
10	25.5
11	28.0
12	30.5
13	33.0

Temperatures

Fahrenheit	Celsius
32°	0°
212°	100°
250°	120°
275°	140°
300°	150°
325°	160°
350°	180°
375°	190°
400°	200°
425°	220°
450°	230°
475°	240°
500°	260°

Weight

U.S. Units	Canadian Metric	Australian Metric
1 ounce	30 grams	30 grams
2 ounces	55 grams	60 grams
3 ounces	85 grams	90 grams
4 ounces (1/4 pound)	115 grams	125 grams
8 ounces (1/2 pound)	225 grams	225 grams
16 ounces (1 pound)	455 grams	500 grams
1 pound	455 grams	1/2 kilogram

Note: The recipes in this cookbook have not been developed or tested using metric measures. When converting recipes to metric, some variations in quality may be noted.

Index

Note: *Italicized* references indicate photographs.

A

Alfredo Salmon and Noodles, 52, *53*
Angel cake, raspberry-filled, 198, *199*
Angel Hair Pasta in Garlic Sauce, 51
Apple(s)
    -butter pork chops, skillet, 95
    cider glaze, chicken with, 134, *135*
    pork chops and, 124, *125*
Apricot bars, creamy frozen, 212
Autumn Grilled Chicken, 156

B

Bacon
    Canadian, and Gouda salad, 26
    in Florentine Salad, 24
    in Quick BLT Salad, 25
    in Spaghetti Carbonara, 42
Bagel pizzas, easy, 89
Bagel sandwiches, honey-ham, 64
Baked Corn on the Cob with Herbs,
    178, *179*
Banana, peanut butter and, wraps, 82
Barbecue
    BBQ Chicken Pizza, 86, *87*
    chicken, sandwiches, quick, 75
    sauce, in Ranchero Beef Pizza, 85
Basil, capellini with lemon and, 54
BBQ Chicken Pizza, 86, *87*
Bean(s)
    black, chicken and, Mexican, 100, *101*
    cannellini, and spinach salad, 33
    great northern, in Slow-Cooker
        Turkey Sausage Cassoulet, 141
    green, and peppers, stir-fried, 186, *187*
    refried, broiled, sandwiches, 76
Beef
    -filled tortellini, vegetable and, soup, 22
    in Greek Lamb and Orzo, 43
    ground, burgers, Coney Island,
        grilled, 167
    ground, burgers, grilled teriyaki, 170
    ground, burgers, jalapeño, 171
    ground, in Southwestern Skillet
        Stroganoff, 40
    'n Cheese Calzone, 84
    pasta, veggies and, cheesy, 36, *37*
    Ranchero, pizza, 85
    in Sloppy Joes with Potatoes and
        Onion, 98
    stir-fried, and vegetable soup, 10
    tips and vegetables, quick, 57
Beets, in Red Summer Soup, 17
Bisque, tomato, easy dilled, 16

Bisquick, in Breaded Pork Chops, 92, *93*
Black-eyed peas, slow-cooker spicy, 185
BLT salad, quick, 25
Blueberry Chicken, 157
Blue Cheese Turkey Burgers, 172, *173*
Bowls, bread, vegetable chowder in,
    20, *21*
Bow-Ties with Turkey, Pesto and
    Roasted Red Peppers, 48, *49*
Bratwurst
    German potato salad with, 23
    and sauerkraut, 96
Bread bowls, vegetable chowder in,
    20, *21*
Breaded Pork Chops, 92, *93*
Broiled Bean Sandwiches, 76
Burgers
    grilled Coney Island, 167
    grilled teriyaki, 170
    Italian, 168, *169*
    jalapeño, 171
    Oriental Turkey Patties, 142, *143*
    Sloppy Joes with Potatoes and
        Onion, 98
    turkey, blue cheese, 172, *173*
    turkey, grilled Texas, 174, *175*
Butter, rosemary-garlic, leeks with, 183

C

Cabbage, in Red Summer Soup, 17
Cake
    angel, creamy raspberry-filled, 198, *199*
    cherry ribbon, slices, 209
Calzone, beef 'n cheese, 84
Canadian Bacon and Gouda Salad, 26
Cantaloupe Sorbet, 208
Capellini with Lemon and Basil, 54
Caramelized-Onion Focaccia Wedges, 77
Caramelized onions, pork with, 94
Carbonara, spaghetti, 42
Carrots
    dilled, and pea pods, 181
    honey-glazed, 182
    in Honey Mustard Turkey with Snap
        Peas, 112, *113*
    in Savory Chicken and Rice, 58
Casserole
    fiesta taco, 130
    lentil and brown rice, 146
    ravioli, microwave, 147
Cassoulet, turkey sausage, slow-cooker,
    141
Chayote, in Vegetable Tortillas, 83

Cheese
    blue, turkey burgers, 172, *173*
    Cheddar, in BBQ Chicken Pizza,
        86, *87*
    Cheddar, in Broiled Bean
        Sandwiches, 76
    Cheddar, in Cheesy Pasta, Veggies and
        Beef, 36, *37*
    Cheddar, in Ranchero Beef Pizza, 85
    Gouda, Canadian bacon and, salad, 26
    grilled, sandwiches, double-decker,
        78, *79*
    Havarti, in Ravioli with Peppers and
        Sun-Dried Tomatoes, 56
    Mexican blend, in Chili Rice
        con Queso, 145
    Mexican blend, in Fiesta Taco
        Casserole, 130
    in Microwave Ravioli Casserole, 147
    Monterey Jack, in Chicken
        Quesadillas, 68, *69*
    Monterey Jack, in Vegetable Tortillas, 83
    Monterey Jack, pizza, 88
    mozzarella and tomato melts, 81
    mozzarella, in Easy Bagel Pizzas, 89
    mozzarella, in Italian Vegetable
        Focaccia Sandwich, 80
    mozzarella, in Pizza Dogs, 66, *67*
    Mozzarella-Topped Chicken and
        Eggplant, 104
    Parmesan, in Spaghetti Carbonara, 42
    Parmesan salad mix, in Zesty Pasta
        Sausage Salad, 29
    shredded, beef 'n, calzone, 84
    smoked, penne with tomato and, 55
    spread, in Warm Hot Dog Pasta
        Salad, 28
Cherry(ies)
    dried, and turkey rice pilaf, 59
    pie filling, in Easy Fruit Crisp
        "Dump" Dessert, 200
    ribbon cake slices, 209
Chicken
    autumn grilled, 156
    barbecue sandwiches, quick, 75
    and beans, Mexican, easy, 100, *101*
    BBQ, pizza, 86, *87*
    blueberry, 157
    breasts, honey-glazed, 133
    chili, spicy, 15
    with cider glaze, 134, *135*
    cordon bleu chowder, 12, *13*
    and eggplant, mozzarella-topped, 104

Chicken *(cont.)*
  and fettuccine, garden, 44, *45*
  garden vegetables, and pasta salad, 46, *47*
  honey-mustard, sandwiches, 74
  lemon-pistachio, 102, *103*
  maple- and cranberry-glazed, 160
  Mediterranean skillet, 99
  oven-fried, crunchy, 136, *137*
  peppery horseradish, 161
  pesto-, packets, 162, *163*
  in Philly Turkey Panini, 72, *73*
  potatoes and, one-pan, 106, *107*
  quesadillas, 68, *69*
  ranch dressing and, 105
  and rice, savory, 58
  rosemary-mustard, 140
  salad, 30, *31*
  skillet-fried, 108, *109*
  sub, hot, 70, *71*
  and summer fruit kabobs, 158, *159*
  teriyaki, stir-fry, 110
  tortellini with portabella mushroom sauce, 50
  two-mustard, 138, *139*
  vegetable-, stir-fry, 111
Chili
  chicken, spicy, 15
  in Fiesta Taco Casserole, 130
  rice con queso, 145
Chocolate cookies, munchy, 205
Chocolate mousse, frozen, 210, *211*
Chowder
  chicken cordon bleu, 12, *13*
  vegetable, in bread bowls, 20, *21*
Cider glaze, chicken with, 134, *135*
Coleslaw, ham and, salad, 27
Coney Island burgers, grilled, 167
Cookies
  chocolate, munchy, 205
  peanut butter, old-fashioned, 206, *207*
Corn
  in Easy Mexican Chicken and Beans, 100, *101*
  on the cob, baked, with herbs, 178, *179*
  salad, zesty, 180
  in Sautéed Polenta, 60
Cornflakes cereal, in Crunchy Oven-Fried Chicken, 136, *137*
Cornmeal, in Sautéed Polenta, 60
Cranberry-, maple-glazed chicken, 160
Creamy Frozen Apricot Bars, 212
Creamy mint sauce, lamb with, 131
Creamy Raspberry-Filled Angel Cake, 198, *199*
Crisp, fruit, "dump" dessert, easy, 200
Crunchy Oven-Fried Chicken, 136, *137*

D
Dill, lemon-, shrimp, 117
Dilled Carrots and Pea Pods, 181
Dilled tomato bisque, easy, 16
Double-Decker Grilled Cheese Sandwiches, 78, *79*
Dried Cherries and Turkey Rice Pilaf, 59

E
Easy Bagel Pizza, 89
Easy Dilled Tomato Bisque, 16
Easy Fruit Crisp "Dump" Dessert, 200
Easy Mexican Chicken and Beans, 100, *101*
Eggplant, chicken and, mozzarella-topped, 104
Eggs, in Florentine Salad, 24

F
Fettuccine
  garden chicken and, 44, *45*
  sausage with, 41
Fiesta Taco Casserole, 130
Fish fillets, panfried, 118
Florentine Salad, 24
Focaccia
  caramelized-onion, wedges, 77
  sandwich, Italian vegetable, 80
4 Star Ideas
  around the world in a salad bowl, 8
  burger bar, 148
  fast and flavorful stir-fries, 90
  fruitful desserts, 196
  great grilling tips, 148
  make-in-minutes marinades, 120
  meal in a potato, 176
  microwave magic, 176
  pastabilities, 34
  personalized pizza, 62
  pound cake dippers, 196
  rice to the rescue, 34
  sandwich savvy, 62
  saucy ideas, 90
  sensational soups, 8
  sundae toppers, 196
  top-notch casseroles, 120
Fried chicken
  oven-fried, crunchy, 136, *137*
  skillet-, 109, *110*
Frozen Chocolate Mousse, 210, *211*
Fruit. *See also specific types*
  crisp "dump" dessert, easy, 200
  kabobs, chicken and, 158, *159*
  salad, in Ham and Slaw Salad, 27

G
Garden Chicken and Fettuccine, 44, *45*
Garden Vegetables, Chicken and Pasta Salad, 46, *47*
Garlic sauce, angel hair pasta in, 51
Garlic Shrimp, 116
German Potato Salad with Brats, 23
Ginger, sesame-, turkey slices, grilled, 164
Glaze, cider, chicken with, 134, *135*
Glazed Country Ribs, 150
Glazed Turkey Tenderloins, 114
Gouda cheese, Canadian bacon and, salad, 26
Greek Lamb and Orzo, 43
Green beans, in Zesty Pasta Sausage Salad, 29
Grilled cheese, sandwiches, double-decker, 78, *79*
Grilled Coney Island Burgers, 167
Grilled Lamb Chops, 153
Grilled main dishes, 150–174
Grilled Salmon with Mint Marinade, 166
Grilled Sesame-Ginger Turkey Slices, 164
Grilled Southwestern Pork Chops, 151
Grilled Steak with Parsley Pesto, 154, *155*
Grilled Teriyaki Burgers, 170
Grilled Texas Turkey Burgers, 174, *175*
Guacamole, in Chicken Quesadillas, 68, *69*

H
Halibut, oven-poached, 144
Ham
  honey-, bagel sandwiches, 64
  and slaw salad, 27
Hoagie, sausage, sizzling, 65
Home-Style Potato Soup, 18, *19*
Honey-Glazed Carrots, 182
Honey-Glazed Chicken Breasts, 133
Honey-Ham Bagel Sandwiches, 64
Honey-Mustard Chicken Sandwiches, 74
Honey Mustard Turkey with Snap Peas, 112, *113*
Honey Sundaes, 213
Horseradish chicken, peppery, 161
Horseradish Mashed Potatoes, 188, *189*
Hot Chicken Sub, 70, *71*
Hot dog(s)
  pasta salad, warm, 28
  pizza, 66, *67*
  in Sizzling Sausage Hoagie, 65

I

Ice. *See also* Sorbet
  lemon, 214
  pineapple, 215
Irish Lamb Stew, 11
Italian Burgers, 168, *169*
Italian Roasted Pork Tenderloin, 126
Italian Sausage Skillet, 97
Italian Vegetable Focaccia Sandwich, 80

J

Jalapeño Burgers, 171

L

Lamb
  chops, grilled, 153
  chops, mustard, 132
  chops, with creamy mint sauce, 131
  ground, orzo and, Greek, 43
  stew, Irish, 11
Leeks with Rosemary-Garlic Butter, 183
Lemon
  capellini with basil and, 54
  -dill shrimp, 117
  ice, 214
  -pistachio chicken, 102, *103*
  spareribs, sweet, 152
Lentil and Brown Rice Casserole, 146
Lettuce, in Quick BLT Salad, 25
Lobster Roast, 165

M

Maple- and Cranberry-Glazed Chicken, 160
Maple-Glazed Turkey Breast, 115
Marinade, mint, grilled salmon with, 166
Marsala sauce, strawberries with, 202, *203*
Mashed potatoes, horseradish, 188, *189*
Meatballs, pasta and, one-pan, 38, *39*
Mediterranean Skillet Chicken, 99
Melts, mozzarella and tomato, 81
Mexican chicken and beans, easy, 100, *101*
Microwave Ravioli Casserole, 147
Mint marinade, grilled salmon with, 166
Mint sauce, creamy, lamb with, 131
Monterey Jack. *See* Cheese
Mousse, chocolate, frozen, 210, *211*
Mozzarella. *See* Cheese
Munchy Chocolate Cookies, 205
Mushroom(s)
  in Beef 'n Cheese Calzone, 84
  in Italian Sausage Skillet, 97
  portabella, sauce, chicken tortellini with, 50
  in Roasted Vegetables, 184
  in Savory Chicken and Rice, 58

Mustard
  honey-, chicken sandwiches, 74
  honey, turkey, with snap peas, 112, *113*
  lamb chops, 132
  rosemary-, chicken, 140
  two-, chicken, 138, *139*

N

Noodle(s)
  chicken, soup, Oriental-style, 14
  Ramen Stir-Fry, 119
  salmon and, Alfredo sauce with, 52, *53*
Nuts, pistachio, lemon-, chicken, 102, *103*

O

Old-Fashioned Peanut Butter Cookies, 206, *207*
One-Pan Pasta and Meatballs, 38, *39*
One-Pan Potatoes and Chicken, 106, *107*
Onion(s)
  caramelized-, focaccia wedges, 77
  caramelized, pork with, 94
  potatoes and, sloppy Joes with, 98
Oriental-Style Chicken Noodle Soup, 14
Oriental Turkey Patties, 142, *143*
Orzo, Greek lamb and, 43
Oven-fried chicken, crunchy, 136, *137*
Oven-Poached Halibut, 144

P

Panfried Fish Fillets, 118
Panini, Philly turkey, 72, *73*
Pantry planner, 6–7
Parmesan. *See* Cheese
Parsley pesto, grilled steak with, 154, *155*
Parsley Potatoes, 190, *191*
Pasta. *See also specific types*
  angel hair, in garlic sauce, 51
  Bow-Ties with Turkey, Pesto and Roasted Red Peppers, 48, *49*
  Capellini with Lemon and Basil, 54
  garden vegetables, chicken and, 46, *47*
  Greek Lamb and Orzo, 43
  and meatballs, one-pan, 38, *39*
  Penne with Tomato and Smoked Cheese, 55
  Ravioli with Peppers and Sun-Dried Tomatoes, 56
  salad, hot dog, warm, 28
  salad, in Quick BLT Salad, 25
  sausage salad, zesty, 29
  in Southwestern Skillet Stroganoff, 40
  Spaghetti Carbonara, 42
  veggies, and beef, cheesy, 36, *37*
Patties, turkey, Oriental, 142, *143*

Pea(s)
  black-eyed, slow-cooker spicy, 185
  pods, carrots and, dilled, 181
  snap, honey mustard turkey with, 112, *113*
Peanut Butter and Banana Wraps, 82
Peanut butter cookies, 206, *207*
Pears
  in Grilled Autumn Chicken, 156
  with raspberry sauce, 201
Penne with Tomato and Smoked Cheese, 55
Pepper(s), bell
  in Italian Sausage Skillet, 97
  in One-Pan Potatoes and Chicken, 106, *107*
  ravioli with sun-dried tomatoes and, 56
  roasted, bow-ties with turkey, pesto and, 48, *49*
  in Roasted Vegetables, 184
  in Sausage with Fettuccine, 41
  stir-fried green beans and, 186, *187*
  in Vegetable Tortillas, 83
  in Warm Bean and Spinach Salad, 33
Peppery Horseradish Chicken, 161
Pesto
  bow-ties with turkey, roasted red peppers, and, 48, *49*
  -chicken packets, 162, *163*
  parsley, grilled steak with, 154, *155*
Philly Turkey Panini, 72, *73*
Pilaf, rice, dried cherries and turkey, 59
Pimientos, in Slow-Cooker Scalloped Potatoes, 193
Pineapple, in Easy Fruit Crisp "Dump" Dessert, 200
Pineapple Ice, 215
Pistachio, lemon-, chicken, 102, *103*
Pizza
  bagel, easy, 89
  BBQ chicken, 86, *87*
  dogs, 66, *67*
  Monterey, 88
  Ranchero beef, 85
Polenta, sautéed, 60
Pork. *See also* Bacon; Ham; Sausage
  chops, breaded, 92, *93*
  chops, grilled Southwestern, 151
  chops, skillet apple-butter, 95
  chops, yummy, 128
  chops and apples, 124, *125*
  roast, garlic, slow-cooker, 122, *123*
  tenderloin with rosemary, 127
  tenderloin, roasted, Italian, 126
  tenderloin, with caramelized onions, 94

Portabella mushroom sauce, chicken
tortellini with, 50
Potato(es)
and chicken, one-pan, 106, *107*
mashed, horseradish, 188, *189*
and onion, sloppy Joes with, 98
parsley, 190, *191*
red, roasted, 192
and sausage supper, scalloped,
slow-cooker, 129
salad, with brats, German, 23
scalloped, slow-cooker, 193
soup, home-style, 18, *19*
sweet, slices, 194
twice-baked, 195

Q

Quesadillas, chicken, 68, *69*
Quick Beef Tips and Vegetables, 57
Quick BLT Salad, 25
Quick Chicken Barbecue Sandwiches, 75

R

Ramen Stir-Fry, 119
Ranch Chicken, 105
Ranchero Beef Pizza, 85
Raspberry(ies)
-filled angel cake, creamy, 198, *199*
frozen, in Red Summer Soup, 17
sauce, pears with, 201
Ravioli, beef, casserole, microwave, 147
Ravioli with Peppers and Sun-Dried
Tomatoes, 56
Red Summer Soup, 17
Ribbon cake, cherry, slices, 209
Ribs
country, glazed, 150
spareribs, sweet lemon, 152
Rice
brown, lentil and, casserole, 146
chicken and, savory, 58
chili, con queso, 145
in Quick Beef Tips and Vegetables, 57
pilaf, dried cherries and turkey, 59
Sautéed Polenta, 60
vegetable-, skillet, 61
Roast, lobster, 165
Roast, pork, garlic, slow-cooker, 122,
123
Roasted pork tenderloin, Italian, 126
Roasted Red Potatoes, 192
Roasted Vegetables, 184
Romanoff, strawberries, 204
Rosemary, pork tenderloin with, 127
Rosemary-garlic butter, leeks with, 183
Rosemary-Mustard Chicken, 140

S

Salad
bean and spinach, warm, 33
BLT, quick, 25
Canadian bacon and Gouda, 26
chicken, 30, *31*
corn, zesty, 180
Florentine, 24
garden vegetables, chicken and pasta,
46, *47*
ham and slaw, 27
pasta sausage, zesty, 29
pasta, hot dog, warm, 28
potato, with brats, German, 23
tuna-vegetable, 32
Salmon, grilled, with mint marinade, 166
Salmon and noodles, Alfredo sauce with,
52, *53*
Salsa
mix, in Chili Rice con Queso, 145
in Southwestern Skillet Stroganoff, 40
Sandwich(es). *See also* Burgers
bagel, honey-ham, 64
bean, broiled, 76
Beef 'n Cheese Calzone, 84
Caramelized-Onion Focaccia
Wedges, 77
chicken barbecue, quick, 75
Chicken Quesadillas, 68, *69*
grilled cheese, double-decker, 78, *79*
honey-mustard chicken, 74
Hot Chicken Sub, 70, *71*
Italian vegetable focaccia, 80
Mozzarella and Tomato Melts, 81
Peanut Butter and Banana Wraps, 82
Philly Turkey Panini, 72, *73*
Pizza Dogs, 66, *67*
Sizzling Sausage Hoagie, 65
Sauce
garlic, angel hair pasta in, 51
marsala, strawberries with, 202, *203*
mint, creamy, lamb with, 131
portabella mushroom, chicken
tortellini, 50
raspberry, pears with, 201
Sauerkraut, bratwurst and, 96
Sausage. *See also* Bratwurst; Hot dog
with fettuccine, 41
hoagie, sizzling, 65
Italian, ravioli, with peppers and
sun-dried tomatoes, 56
Italian, skillet, 97
pasta, salad, zesty, 29
potato and, supper, scalloped,
slow-cooker, 129
turkey, cassoulet, slow-cooker, 141

Sautéed Polenta, 60
Savory Chicken and Rice, 58
Scalloped potato and sausage supper,
slow-cooker, 129
SuperExpress recipes
Angel Hair Pasta in Garlic Sauce, 51
BBQ Chicken Pizza, 86, *87*
Bow-Ties with Turkey, Pesto and
Roasted Red Peppers, 48, *49*
Bratwurst and Sauerkraut, 96
Breaded Pork Chops, 92, *93*
Broiled Bean Sandwiches, 76
Canadian Bacon and Gouda Salad, 26
Capellini with Lemon and Basil, 54
Chicken Cordon Bleu Chowder, 12, *13*
Chicken Salad, 30, *31*
Chicken Tortellini with Portabella
Mushroom Sauce, 50
Dilled Carrots and Pea Pods, 181
Easy Bagel Pizza, 89
Easy Dilled Tomato Bisque, 16
Garden Chicken and Fettucine, 44, *45*
Garlic Shrimp, 116
Greek Lamb and Orzo, 43
Grilled Coney Island Burgers, 167
Grilled Lamb Chops, 153
Grilled Steak with Parsley Pesto, 154,
155
Ham and Slaw Salad, 27
Honey-Ham Bagel Sandwiches, 64
Honey Sundaes, 213
Italian Vegetable Focaccia Sandwich, 80
Lamb with Creamy Mint Sauce, 131
Lemon-Dill Shrimp, 117
Lemon-Pistachio Chicken, 102, *103*
Microwave Ravioli Casserole, 147
Mozzarella and Tomato Melts, 81
Mozzarella-Topped Chicken and
Eggplant, 104
Oriental-Style Chicken Noodle
Soup, 14
Peanut Butter and Banana Wraps, 82
Philly Turkey Panini, 72, *73*
Pizza Dogs, 66, *67*
Quick Beef Tips and Vegetables, 57
Quick Chicken Barbecue
Sandwiches, 75
Ranch Chicken, 105
Ravioli with Peppers and Sun-Dried
Tomatoes, 56
Sausage with Fettuccine, 41
Southwestern Skillet Stroganoff, 40
Spaghetti Carbonara, 42
Spicy Chicken Chili, 15
Stir-Fried Beef and Vegetable Soup, 10

Stir-Fried Green Beans and Peppers, 186, *187*
Teriyaki Chicken Stir-Fry, 110
Tuna-Vegetable Salad, 32
Vegetable and Tortellini Soup, 22
Vegetable-Chicken Stir-Fry, 111
Vegetable Chowder in Bread Bowls, 20, *21*
Vegetable-Rice Skillet, 61
Warm Bean and Spinach Salad, 33
Zesty Salad Corn, 180
Sesame-ginger turkey slices, grilled, 164
Shrimp
    garlic, 116
    lemon-dill, 117
Sizzling Sausage Hoagie, 65
Skillet, Italian sausage, 97
Skillet, vegetable-rice, 61
Skillet Apple-Butter Pork Chops, 95
Skillet chicken, Mediterranean, 99
Skillet-Fried Chicken, 108, *109*
Skillet main dishes, 92–119
Skillet stroganoff, southwestern, 40
Slaw, ham and, salad, 27
Sloppy Joes with Potatoes and Onion, 98
Slow-Cooker Garlic Pork Roast, 122, *123*
Slow-Cooker Scalloped Potato and Sausage Supper, 129
Slow-Cooker Scalloped Potatoes, 193
Slow-Cooker Spicy Black-Eyed Peas, 185
Slow-Cooker Turkey Sausage Cassoulet, 141
Sorbet, cantaloupe, 208
Soup. *See also* Stew
    bisque, tomato, dilled, easy, 16
    chicken noodle, Oriental-style, 14
    chowder, chicken cordon bleu, 12, *13*
    chowder, vegetable, in bread bowls, 20, *21*
    potato, home-style, 18, *19*
    red summer, 17
    stir-fried beef and vegetable, 10
    vegetable and tortellini, 22
Southwestern pork chops, grilled, 151
Southwestern Skillet Stroganoff, 40
Spaghetti Carbonara, 42
Spicy Chicken Chili, 15
Spinach
    bean and, salad, warm, 33
    in Florentine Salad, 24
    in Vegetable and Tortellini Soup, 22

Steak, T-bone, grilled, with parsley pesto, 154, *155*
Stew, Irish lamb, 11
Stir-fry(ied)
    beef and vegetable soup, 10
    green beans and peppers, 186, *187*
    ramen, 119
    teriyaki chicken, 110
    vegetable-chicken, 111
Strawberries Romanoff, 204
Strawberries with Marsala Sauce, 202, *203*
Stroganoff, southwestern skillet, 40
Sundaes, honey, 213
Sweet Lemon Spareribs, 152
Sweet Potato Slices, 194

T
Taco casserole, fiesta, 130
Taco seasoning mix, in Easy Mexican Chicken and Beans, 100, *101*
Teriyaki burgers, grilled, 170
Teriyaki Chicken Stir-Fry, 110
Texas turkey burgers, grilled, 174, *175*
Tomato(es)
    bisque, easy dilled, 16
    diced, in Chili Rice con Queso, 12
    in Mediterranean Skillet Chicken, 99
    mozzarella and, melts, 81
    in Quick BLT Salad, 25
    sauce, garlic-and-herb, in Sausage with Fettuccine, 41
    sauce, in Mozzarella-Topped Chicken and Eggplant, 104
    sauce, in Sausage with Fettuccini, 41
    and smoked cheese, penne with, 55
    stewed, in Pasta: Greek Lamb and Orzo, 43
    sun-dried, ravioli with peppers and, 56
Tortellini
    chicken, with portabella mushroom sauce, 50
    in Tuna-Vegetable Salad, 32
    vegetable and, soup, 22
Tortillas
    in Chicken Quesadillas, 68, *69*
    in Peanut Butter and Banana Wraps, 82
    vegetable, 83
Tuna-Vegetable Salad, 32

Turkey
    bow-ties, pesto, roasted red peppers, and, 48, *49*
    breast, maple-glazed, 115
    burgers, blue cheese, 172, *173*
    burgers, grilled Texas, 174, *175*
    in Chicken Salad, 30, *31*
    dried cherries and, rice pilaf, 59
    ground, in Italian Burgers, 168, *169*
    honey mustard, with snap peas, 112, *113*
    panini, Philly, 72, *73*
    patties, Oriental, 142, *143*
    sausage cassoulet, slow-cooker, 141
    slices, grilled sesame-ginger, 164
    tenderloins, glazed, 114
Twice-Baked Potatoes, 195
Two-Mustard Chicken, 138, *139*

V
Vegetable(s). *See also specific types*
    -chicken stir-fry, 111
    chowder in bread bowls, 20, *21*
    focaccia sandwich, Italian, 80
    garden, chicken and pasta salad, 46, *47*
    pasta, and beef, cheesy, 36, *37*
    in Pizza Monterey, 88
    quick beef tips and, 57
    -rice skillet, 61
    roasted, 184
    stir-fried beef and, soup, 10
    in Teriyaki Chicken Stir-Fry, 110
    and tortellini soup, 22
    tortillas, 83
    tuna-, salad, 32

W
Warm Bean and Spinach Salad, 33
Warm Hot Dog Pasta Salad, 28
Water chestnuts, in Oriental Turkey Patties, 142, *143*
Wraps, peanut butter and banana, 82

Y
Yummy Pork Chops, 128

Z
Zesty Pasta Sausage Salad, 29
Zesty Salad Corn, 180
Zucchini
    in Pesto-Chicken Packets, 162, *163*
    in Roasted Vegetables, 184

Complete your cookbook library
with these *Betty Crocker* titles

Betty Crocker's Best Bread Machine Cookbook
Betty Crocker's Best Chicken Cookbook
Betty Crocker's Best Christmas Cookbook
Betty Crocker's Best of Baking
Betty Crocker's Best of Healthy and Hearty Cooking
Betty Crocker's Best-Loved Recipes
Betty Crocker's Bisquick® Cookbook
Betty Crocker's Bread Machine Cookbook
Betty Crocker's Cook It Quick
Betty Crocker's Cookbook, 9th Edition - *The* **BIG RED** *Cookbook*®
Betty Crocker's Cookbook, Bridal Edition
Betty Crocker's Cookie Book
Betty Crocker's Cooking for Two
Betty Crocker's Cooky Book, Facsimile Edition
Betty Crocker's Cooking Basics
Betty Crocker's Diabetes Cookbook
Betty Crocker's Easy Slow Cooker Dinners
Betty Crocker's Eat and Lose Weight
Betty Crocker's Entertaining Basics
Betty Crocker's Flavors of Home
Betty Crocker's Great Grilling
Betty Crocker's Healthy New Choices
Betty Crocker's Indian Home Cooking
Betty Crocker's Italian Cooking
Betty Crocker's Kids Cook!
Betty Crocker's Kitchen Library
Betty Crocker's Living with Cancer
Betty Crocker's Low-Fat Low-Cholesterol Cooking Today
Betty Crocker's New Cake Decorating
Betty Crocker's New Chinese Cookbook
Betty Crocker's A Passion for Pasta
Betty Crocker's Picture Cook Book, Facsimile Edition
Betty Crocker's Quick & Easy Cookbook
Betty Crocker's Slow Cooker Cookbook
Betty Crocker's Ultimate Cake Mix Cookbook
Betty Crocker's Vegetarian Cooking